Journey Through Life

by
Galina Cherubin

1663 LIBERTY DRIVE, SUITE 200
BLOOMINGTON, INDIANA 47403
(800) 839-8640
WWW.AUTHORHOUSE.COM

© 2005 Galina Cherubin. All Rights Reserved.

No part of this book may be reproduced, stored in a retrieval system, or transmitted by any means without the written permission of the author.

First published by AuthorHouse 10/31/05

ISBN: 1-4208-7762-3 (sc)

Library of Congress Control Number: 2005907346

Printed in the United States of America
Bloomington, Indiana

This book is printed on acid-free paper.

Table of Contents

Part I In the Jaws of Red Dragon 1
   I. Introduction 3
   II. Broken Childhood! 8
   III. "Free, But Not Free"… 14
   IV. Free from Stalin's camp, but not completely free yet… 24
   V. Childhood in the Socialist camp 26
   VI. My Summer Adventures 28
   VII. My First Election 30
   VIII. New Year's Eve 32
   IX. Our Trip To Tallinn 37
   X. My brother's childhood friend 46
   XI. The Grechko Family 57
   XII. A Summer Job… 65
   XIII. Teens in the Army of Christ 68
   XIV. Friends in the Soviet Army 72
   XV. Sunday Morning Vision 74
   XVI. Meeting with the Diplomats and Consul 76
   XVII. Boris 79
   XVIII. Wandering in the Woods 89
   XIX. Maria Phedorovna – A Prayer in the Kitchen 93
   XX. Demonstration of Protest 96
   XXI. The Trip to Brest 103
   XXII. A Surprise Good-bye Party 106
   XXIII. An Unexpected Chase 108
   XXIV. Crossing the "Red Sea" 110

Part II New World 115
   XXV. Adapting to the New World 117
   XXVI. The Speech at Pennsylvania University 122
   XXVII. My Important Friends 124
   XXVIII. My Working Career Continues 134
   XXIX. In a Search for the Other Half 137
   XXX. Memories of the Past 154
   XXXI. My Life Is Making An Amazing Turn 162
   XXXII. Reaction of My Family 167
   XXXIII. Rejected by the Church 170
   XXXIV. The Big Wedding Day 174
   XXXV. Family Life 179
   XXXVI. All the Troubles Come at Once 183
   XXXVII. Back To Low Income 189
   XXXVIII. Masha & Serezha 193
   XXXIX. An Important Messenger 198
   XL. Pregnant Again! 204
   XLI. September 11 207
   XLII. Down The Hill Once Again 210
   XLIII. Busy Winter 218
   XLIV. Coming To Florida 225
   XLV. He Is Never Late! 227
   XLVI. Happy Ending 233
   XLVII. The Final Chapter Before
The Conclusion 237
   XLVIII. Conclusion 249
   XLIX. A Prayer for You 253

Part I
In the Jaws
of Red Dragon

I. Introduction

"Who will tell me the ten thesis of the October Revolution?" Anatoly Demidovich thoroughly looked at the class. He let a few minutes to go by for the students to sort out their answers.

"Anybody? I need to see hands…" The class became very quiet for a few minutes. Everybody was looking through the pages of the History book.

"Did you do your homework yesterday? It doesn't look like you came prepared for your class today," we heard a note of disappointment in the voice of the teacher.

"Anatoly Demidovich, don't you remember that we had to do the community work around the school?" my classmate Peter, who sat on my right screwed up enough courage to reply to the teacher.

"I came home so tired that I wasn't able to do my homework well. Please give me another chance. This will not happen again."

"That's right, that's right," was heard from everywhere, "we had no chance to do it yesterday…"

"All right, class, please calm down, I am convinced. I am going to repeat yesterday's topic again, but I would like you to listen with your full attention, because tomorrow I will not accept any excuses. The first thesis of the Revolution was to take all the land from the kulaks (rich peasants) and pass the ownership to all people. That's what Commune is about – land for people. Everybody would have an equal share of all the treasures that our country possesses…"

Anatoly Demidovich was going on and on… His steady voice put me into a deep thinking. I didn't hear anything else from that history topic, my mind was floating far away from what Anatoly Demidovich could offer.

Everything that they ever said in the school was so different from real life. History class was not about real history at all, it was just a boring subject about Lenin, Revolution, Communism and the distorted information about Capitalism. Teachers had to fill children's minds with all kinds of "garbage" so they would not ask real questions.

Shame on you, servants of evil, look around and get real! This is the twentieth century; the century of great developments, discoveries and a tremendous increase of intelligence. This is the century of celebration of the human mind! However, to our shame, many of the things I remember I wish had never happened. For example, humanity would be much happier if Hitler was never born and never killed an enormous number of innocent people. I wished that the Holocaust never took place during the Second World War and Jewish bodies never have been used in the place of firewood. I wish that Lenin never took people's minds and tricked them into Communism. Communism is a system that was designed to slowly destroy people's minds, otherwise, people's bodies, and turn them into piles of ashes. I would define Communism as a ruthless human-eating machine that would swallow everyone without mercy. Those who refused to be swallowed would be crushed with its powerful canines. There is nothing in the world that could fight with the system of the RED BEAST, except God. God is the only power that can fight any of the evil-founding empires. The former Soviet Union was one of the empires that celebrated the devil instead of God. Furthermore, they were very proud of calling themselves a nation without God. "There is no God, we are gods ourselves," they used to proclaim. "Well, the devil exists and we are worshipping him delightfully, because the devil gives POWER! The definitions of evil and good could be turned around, depending on how you look at them. "Good" is a weak feature and usually sticks to weak-minded people. The real power is always behind the one who is stronger, and evil always wins whether you agree or not! Therefore, evil is a powerful victory, this is the law of the world and this will never change. If the devil didn't have power, we wouldn't be as strong!" This ideology was pushed into every person's mind, no matter of the age. Communists were trying to "educate" everyone, especially children, because a child's brain will absorb everything it gets.

I was getting this kind of "education" starting from elementary school. However, my parents had already done some teaching about God, which was absolutely opposite to the Communist doctrine. At my young age I learned to trust my parents more than the teachers at my school. This helped me resist ungodly theory. I was yelled at by the teachers, and had to resist the anger of my principal, who was hitting the table with his steel fists, I was approached in many ways by the authorities that were trying to clear my head from Jesus. In spite of being an excellent student of the school, I was denied higher education, because of my belief in God. The shadow of persecution was following me throughout my entire childhood. I was dreaming about the place in the world where children had an equal value in the society. I was building up anger against the cruel system that was making people mentally handicapped. At my early years I was dreaming about Canada, where I had a distant family. My father's cousin would mail us pictures from Canada. I enjoyed looking at those color photos where I would see my aunt, uncle and their two children. They looked so beautiful on the pictures, all dressed up in such outfits that I couldn't even dream of getting. I would get a little jealous about them. "Why couldn't I be in a beautiful place like my cousins, why did I have to be born in a country that wouldn't let me be happy? Why do all these mean adults yell at me all the time, just because I worship God?"

One day I asked my mother to let me write a letter to my Canadian aunt. She said, "All right." I wrote the best letter I could write as a child. In my letter I asked my aunt to send me some of those nice clothes that I saw on the pictures. My aunt was a very compassionate woman and she replied very fast with a package of beautiful dresses that I would never forget in my life. Beautifully printed flowers on chiffon trimmed with lace brightened up my day and my whole childhood. Every time I felt sad and rejected by other children, I would remember those dresses and that would cheer me up. They were my special lucky charms. My Canadian aunt sent us a few more packages, and all of them were considered to be as valuable as gold in my immature child's mind. Those packages strengthened my dream of going to Canada.

For many nights I would dream about beautiful Canadian gardens full of unspeakably charming flowers, and I would walk from flower to flower and smell their heavenly aroma. I would chase and catch butterflies, and would look into the pond. I would enjoy the flower-crown in my hair and sparkling turquoise dress. Just as I started to walk around the garden, I woke up in my old bed as my sister pushed me with her knee. Realizing that my wonderful experience was just a dream, I was very disappointed. Many times I day-dreamed and promised myself that when I grow up, I would find a way to come out of this awful country that takes away childhood from Christian kids like me. I was growing up, but the desire to fight back never faded away from my mind. On the contrary, it was growing stronger.

The day had come when I became a soldier of Christ. I stood for my beliefs and fought for my Christian rights and the religious freedom within "the jaws of the Red Dragon".

The first part of the book "In the Jaws of Red Dragon" is inspired by true stories that happened in my life and lives of my family and friends who crossed under the knives of the Soviet regime. The second part of the book, "New World", is about how I adapted to the United States. It tells you about my achievements and failures, my happy moments and tragedies, romantic love and marriage, excitements and disappointments; and how God works everything for good for those who love Him.

This book is dedicated to the lovely memory of my father who survived Hitler's war, Stalin's reign, and the most extreme edges of the Communist system. However, the beast ruined my father's health and he passed away in nineteen ninety-six, but died in the free land of America.

II. Broken Childhood!

Once upon a time, when my father was a ten-year-old boy, Hitler moved his army to the territory of Poland and Belarus. A little peaceful town (it used to be on Polish territory, but after the war it was occupied by the Soviet Union and was officially declared a Belarussian town) was turned into a battlefield. It is kind of hard to describe life under a war. Actually, you couldn't call it life… it was a fight for survival. The war simplified all the laws: the strongest always wins, the weak one loses the battle. Loosing a battle during a war meant loosing a life. Elderly, women, children, handicapped… there were no exceptions – everyone was under the obligation to protect himself!

Peter Marchuk, my father, was just a little boy, when the war hit his small village. Unlike his brothers and sisters (he had 6 siblings), he was a weak and unhealthy child. All the illnesses that he had in his childhood slowed down his growth. He was always smaller and weaker than his brothers. One time little Peter overheard his parents' conversation – they were discussing his health issues. "Well", the father was saying to the mother, "I know that my children will get through this war and will make their way in life. However, I don't know what will happen to Peter. He is so small and weak, I don't think he can survive this war." Being just a child, Peter didn't pay much attention to his parents' words, but for some reason he always remembered what his father said that day.

One day Peter was staring in the window, where he could view the whole field in front of his house. The field used to be blooming with beautiful flowers. Peter liked flowers, trees and all the nature that surrounded him in the days of his childhood. But that day the panorama that opened in front of him was significantly different from the usual view. What he saw in the window was not as enjoyable as

Journey Through Life

usual. On the contrary, it was terrifying. There was a group of soldiers carrying rifles on their shoulders and yelling something unclear. My father could recognize that they were Germans. They were accompanied by two Russian men from the village. Russians were copying everything Germans did. They were Russian spies, who switched to the German side and worked for Gestapo. (Peter heard adult conversation about them earlier). The saddest thing about that whole picture was that the soldiers were forcing one of Peter's neighbors out of their house. They dragged everyone out and lined them up on the field. The mother was holding a little infant. Other children hung to her legs, trying to find protection. However, there was no protection or hiding place at the war. They were like a herd of hungry beasts that jump on their prey and tear it apart. Gestapo soldiers yelled a few commands to the scared little children. Unable to line them up, they lifted their guns and started to shoot.

Peter jumped away from the window in fear. He hid his face in a pillow for a few minutes, but the child's curiosity brought him back to the same spot. He heard the voices of the soldiers yelling something in German. It seemed like it meant, "Shoot them and finish the job", because six gunshots followed those words. Peter heard the desperate voices of the mother and children begging for mercy, but there was no mercy in the glass eyes of the cold-blooded murderers. In heartbreaking fear, Peter froze at the window, watching tiny figures falling to the ground. The mother fell down tightly holding her infant, but the baby never stopped crying! Peter saw that the cry of the baby got on the cruel soldiers' nerves, because they started to shoot like crazy. For some reason they couldn't get rid of that desperate cry of the infant. For about five minutes soldiers had been missing their last target, but they finally got it. The last of the prey was shot to death and everything became very quiet. A pile of dead bodies, covered with blood froze in a shadow of death. The

"Bloody operation" was completed. Satisfied with the "job well done", the predators left the scene.

Peter's face was covered with tears and his heart was filled with mixed feelings of rage, fear and desire of revenge. He ran to his mother and was trying to say something, but no words would come out of his mouth. "I know, I know, my sweetheart," whispered his mother trying to calm him down. "We have to kneel down and ask our big Jesus to protect us all." She couldn't talk any more, a loud scream broke out of her chest and she fell down on the bed, weeping and praying.

Many times Peter saw Germans, accompanied by Russian spies, killing peaceful civilians without any reason. There was especially no mercy for the families who had someone in the Russian Army or in the army of "Partisan" (civilian forces). Germans would wipe anyone who was not with them off the face of the earth. The Russian spies had their own fears. They pleased Germans, who were in authority at that time, but they feared Russian "Partisans". It was very tough and tricky for the civilians to figure out who to serve, but the most difficult part of that was the fact that there was no option of being neutral. Everyone under German occupation was living under a constant fear of death.

At times Peter was terrified by the scenes that he had to witness, but there was no alternative except to try your best to stay out of trouble. He was hoping that the day would come when the war would be finished. In his dreams little Peter would find himself in a beautiful field and the sun would be bright, the grass would be really green and the birds would be singing Rock-a-bye songs for him. But the enjoyment would never last, because every morning he would wake up to the terrible reality of the war. In his little age he had to make a living on the battlefield...

One day somebody reported Peter's family to the Gestapo, due to the fact of his uncle serving in the Partisan

Journey Through Life

army. Very early at the sunrise Peter heard voices of the strangers and the knock on the door. When he looked in the window, he recognized the same "bloody team" that he saw through the window two weeks ago. He was terrified! He ran to the furthest corner of the room and hid behind a pile of clothes, but his refuge was discovered very fast. Gestapo soldiers broke into the house and pushed them all out, pointing guns at everyone in the family. "What is the problem, what is happening?" Peter's father was trying to question the furious soldiers. But they were not there to negotiate. They only yelled "Out, out, out! Partisans, out!" Peter figured out that it was something in relation between them and the Partisans. They slowly moved out of the house, one by one.

"Here they were, lined up on the grass in front of mad German soldiers. Where is the justice? Where is the fair judgement? Is there anyone that could hear them and save them from that reprisal? Did they have to die today by being shot by these beasts, just like the other family?" Peter never stopped questioning himself. His heart was beating rapidly at the highest rate, and the blood was pounding in his temples. His face turned red. He was shaking, trembling, and was breathing heavily. Was the world going to close up on him today and will he fall into the eternal shadow of death, from where nobody ever comes back? "Oh, God, can you hear me? Are you going to watch me dying today? Can you perform a miracle and save us?" he was screaming but nobody could hear him. Peter wasn't even sure that God existed, but he had to talk to someone, even if he talked silently.

Suddenly, they heard shots from the nearby forest. Fearing the Partisans, the predators left their prey and ran into the forest. Did they run in fear of their lives or because they were trying to capture the shooter – nobody knew that, the only thing Peter knew was that the murderers ran and left them alone. As soon as the butchers ran far enough,

Peter's father commanded: "Everybody, follow me! Run as fast as you can, don't fall behind!" There was not a moment to be lost! The whole family ran in the opposite direction from the soldiers, trying to reach the other side of the forest. They only slowed down when they found themselves surrounded by trees. They looked back at their house. At this very moment, looking between the trees, Peter saw their enemies, returning back to the house to finish the job. When he realized that death was still-hunting behind them, he kept running along with his family further and further and further! When they thought that they had run far enough they stopped. Peter took a deep breath.

Everything was very quiet; he could hear the rustle of the tree leaves. He looked around once again and understood that he was in the heart of the woods. Nobody could find them there except rabbits, squirrels and other forest inhabitants. Who would find the way there except him, whose soul was merged together with the forest from day one? Peter breathed in the aroma of the surrounding nature. The air was so pure and clean; it seemed to have a double portion of oxygen in it. Peter slowly walked around the trees inhaling the purest air of the generous nature…

"We gotta look for shelter now," said Peter's father, disturbing his peaceful meditation. They found a little cave to hide in. They gathered some tree branches for better comfort and hid inside in fear of being discovered by the enemies. When Peter realized that they escaped death, he started to think that there might be a God. To him their escape was a real miracle, in addition, it was an answer to his short and silent prayer.

Later, Peter found out that there was a God, who was watching over him at that very moment of fear for his life and gave him the opportunity to run and hide until it was safe. They were fugitives of the war, hiding in the forest until it was safe to go back home. Peter accepted Jesus, who was with him and his family during those long years of the war. God wonderfully protected them during that critical time of the fight for survival! May all the praise be to God!

III. "Free, But Not Free"...

The war was finished and the country was rebuilding burnt cities and recultivating the land. However, it took much longer to rebuild broken lives. Four years after the war ended, Peter was called to serve in the Russian Army. This was a mandatory law for every eighteen-year-old boy. Due to being underweight (a minimum weight was required for a soldier - fifty kilograms), he was returned home for another year. When he turned nineteen and caught up with his weight, he was called to serve his two years turn in the army. Peter joined The Soviet Army, but had no idea of what the future held for him. When he found out that he had to swear to Communist principals and to the Russian Red Flag, he realized that it was conflicting with the Biblical principals and with his belief in God. Communism is not just ungodly, but an anti-godly system. This system was made to destroy everything related to God and Christianity. Peter had to choose between God and Communism. Due to being a faithful believer and remembering all the grace and miracles that God performed in his young life, he chose to follow God. He had to pay a high price for his choice, but God never left him alone and gave him the strength to handle all the persecution and tortures that took place throughout his life.

Since Peter refused to follow "the rules", stating that he wouldn't deny God, the army personnel came up with a smart plan to break his spirit.

At first, he was brainwashed for thirty days around the clock. It was a really tough test to be up in front of military court every two hours: two hours of rest, two hours of questioning and so on for the whole month. His schedule looked like a checkerboard: black square, white square, black square, white square... However, it wasn't as fun as a checkers game. Very soon his body got exhausted, his eyes

Journey Through Life

wouldn't stay open; his legs wouldn't obey him. Sometimes he would pass out at the interrogatory sessions, but the "blood-sucking animals" maliciously enjoyed looking at his struggles. They would pour a bucket of water on his head to make him get back to a conscious state. There was no mercy in the desperate builders of Communism. Their motto was "To kill, To destroy, To torture, To make everybody obey and follow!" Their goal was to make obedient human-machines, which won't have a free will and would not resist or refuse any of the Communist ideas. Peter was told that there was no God, but it didn't matter, because he had no choice. The only religion that was considered in The Soviet Union at that time was Communism.

Peter was a tough character with a strong will. He made a promise that nothing would ever break his spirit and nothing would separate him from God. After a month of trial, he was requested to make a choice between God and his life. It was a dreadful demand from the cruel authorities! He was only given one life to live and his life just began...

Peter stayed quiet and for a few minutes he felt a bitter lump in his throat... "What do I do? Jesus, what do I do in this situation?" in despair he was looking for an answer. He looked around the room, but he saw nothing around except three steel faces of the Soviet colonels. Suddenly he felt a warm stream that filled his chest and he heard a voice talking to him from within, "Are you going to deny me? I went on the cross for you and gave my life for your salvation. Don't be afraid, I will never leave you." Peter looked at the colonels in astonishment, but they were just sitting there, silently waiting for his response. "Am I loosing my mind? Who just spoke to me? Am I getting insane after all these trials? The words sounded so real! Jesus," he said, "was that your voice?" In a state of confusion he closed his eyes and silently prayed. He heard the voice again, "Peter, why are you afraid? I am Jesus and I came to answer your prayer. I will be with you during all your trials." All his confusions were suddenly gone and peace descended into his heart. He received an assurance and confidence that replaced all of his fears. God was the One that he wanted to serve; everything else, including his own life, he placed into God's hands. God became the highest authority for him and this was his final decision!

He lifted his head, looked at the colonels and said, "You have the power over my physical body, but you cannot touch my soul, because it doesn't belong to you. It belongs to God." Their red furious faces were looking at him, trying to understand - what drives this skinny soldier from within, what gives him the strength to stand so strongly for his mysterious God?

Full of madness and frustration, they dropped him in a temporary cell and left him alone. He was happy that he finally could be by himself, one-on-one with God and away from his torturers. Peter fell into a deep sleep. He couldn't remember how long he slept, but a few strangers in military uniforms awakened him. They commanded him to follow them. He didn't have to wait long to discover a new approach, designed especially for him. The "crafty heads" of communists worked very hard, creating new methods on how to enslave human minds. He was taken to a military vehicle and they took off. Only God knew where he was going, because he couldn't see anything from the dark uncomfortable cabin. Confused thoughts were going through his head. He simply couldn't make sense out of anything. He was very anxious to find out what was going on. Blindly captured by the enemies, he was just a helpless hostage.

The vehicle was going miles and miles away from his last home, if you could call it home. It was running on such an uneven road that every bump echoed in his ears. He was tossed from side to side in the vehicle, especially, when it ran

Journey Through Life

over large bumps. He felt a heavy blood pulse in his temples, and his stomach felt weak and nauseous. It was like being trapped inside of a huge blender. He wished that they would get there faster, even if he had no idea of what was waiting for him on the other end of the route.

Time was dragging, this road trip was impossibly long, longer than he could take. He was about to scream for help just as the vehicle slowed down and stopped. He was escorted from the cabin by two armed men. The bright light screwed up his eyes. Wow! The sunshine was really powerful! Soon he got used to the brightness of the daylight and found out that he was in a strange place. It was a deserted place in the mountains, never seen by him before. He quietly followed the guards... "Where are we going? Wait a minute! There is no way further! This the end of a cliff!" His face turned pale and he got a little dizzy. The captain's voice awakened him;

"This is it! I am giving you your last chance to make a choice! What is it going to be? Your God or your LIFE?" the captain's lips were moving slowly.

He pulled out a gun and pointed at Peter's face.

"I am going to count to three. Carefully listen to my instructions, I mean it – CAREFULLY! One... Are you willing to give up your God yet?" Peter silently shook his head side to side.

"I am counting, remember that your life is in my hands. Two... Any changes?" "No", Peter whispered.

"Did you just say "NO"? I don't believe it! Do you understand how serious it is? One more refusal and your life will end forever! Don't you understand this!? You will not exist any more! This is your last chance! Three!..."

Everything became quiet for a minute but then the sound of Peter's voice drew all eyes towards him,

"I was, I am and I will be a Christian as long as I breathe."

Galina Cherubin

The angry captain pulled the trigger... Peter closed his eyes and waited...that moment lasted eternity. His whole life passed in front of his eyes... He visualized his family, his noisy brothers and sisters...He traveled through his house and the backyard...He grasped that beautiful smile of his best friend Olga from the photo that hung on the wall...

Then he realized that nothing happened. He opened his eyes and what he saw was a miracle! The captain was madly pulling the trigger, but the gun would not fire! He pressed it again and again, he was loosing his temper, but the gun was silent! Everybody who was invited to watch the scene froze in a silent fear, "What now?"

After a few unsuccessful attempts the captain yelled: "Take him back to the car!" Peter was astonished! He didn't know what was going to happen next, but his heart was rejoicing because he knew exactly who blocked the gun – God, the one that he worshipped! He slowly followed the officers but his heart was celebrating! It was a one-person party; it was hidden from the external eyes, but his internal being was filled with joy!

A week later Peter was brought to a special camp that was designed upon Stalin's request as one of the methods in breaking "Christ followers". There were a lot of them in Siberia and also in the Far East. Peter was placed in the most remote one that was located on the island Sakhalin (an island located near Japan). It was a large restricted open area with hundreds of tents in it. Each tent was made out of a rough cotton fabric with a metal drum in the middle, which was supposed to represent a heater. Wood that was burnt in the drum was giving very poor heat at the very low temperature of –40F. Frozen bodies were thrown in the snow every single day. Dirty liquid with fish heads in it was served as soup for the camp residents during the whole term. All the horrors of camp life were like a never-ending nightmare.

Journey Through Life

Peter was sentenced to five years of such life! If he had to sit down and think of where his life finally brought him, he would probably loose his mind. He saw how some convicts turned completely normal people into the mentally ill individuals. There was nothing that he could do to help these poor fellows. Besides, he had to make his own survival plan. Being completely separated from his family and friends, without getting any correspondence or communication from the outside world Peter was looking for reasons to stay alive, and he found it. His biggest reason was God, who never left him alone. He heard him and answered his prayers. Believing that God has control over his life, Peter tried to keep that peace and composure in his heart, knowing that nobody could enter that holy area of his being.

Day after day watching the life in a camp, he soon was able to recognize the environment that the fellows came from and what experience they had left behind their years. He saw some really rude guys that didn't care about anybody, some who would even step on your throat if you got in their way. There was another group of convicts that wouldn't bother anybody at all, but would try to keep from getting into arguments and fights. As time passed by, Peter found out that there were a few Christians. Over time he even made friends with one of the believers. They would sneak out and pray together while the security was "taking a nap". This fellowship with someone who had the same faith as he had played a huge role in Peter's survival.

One day his friend approached him with some kind of gleam on his face. It was easy to understand that he had news. Peter was looking for an opportunity to speak to with his friend. When they finally got a moment to talk to each other, his friend revealed to him that he had a dream. In his dream an angel appeared in front of him and announced, "Watch what happens on March third, nineteen fifty-three." They looked at each other with a smile, and like a refreshing drink of water, hope enlightened their faces and hearts in this gloomy and dark camp environment. The two friends were patiently waiting to see what would happen on that date, revealed to them by an angel. Day after day, month after month... the friends continued their spiritual relationship, keeping their hopes up that the victorious day will come. They were anxiously counting down to that day, and couldn't wait to see what God was trying to reveal to them.

Finally, the long-awaited day arrived. That morning the two friends looked at each other with puzzled faces. The first half of the day passed ordinarily; everything seemed to be the same: the same gray walls of the camp, the same gloomy faces of the residents, the same lousy food, the same rules, the same commands, etc... A few more frozen bodies were dumped into the snow outside the area. Was that a revelation or just a dream of the freedom-wanting mind of the convicted fellow? Both of them were holding on to their hope. With all the faith that they could possible put together they were watching the life of the camp very closely.

Sometime in the second half of the day, a voice in the megaphone announced a camp meeting. Everybody was commanded to come out of their barracks (camp tents). As soon as Peter heard the announcement, his heart started to beat rapidly in his chest. He knew that this had to be something important. When he went outside, he saw a lot of activities around; prisoners were crowding in-groups, trying to understand what was going on. The guards were running around hoping to make some kind of order out of this noisy crowd. Finally, a voice out of the megaphone made everyone quiet.

"Attention, attention, attention! Today, on March the third, nineteen hundred fifty third year, our country is in a deep mourning! We have lost our father and leader, our General Secretary of Communist Party of the Soviet Union, Joseph Stalin. As of today he went to rest with our fathers.

Journey Through Life

Please bow your heads and show your honor in a minute of silence..."

Everyone took off his hat and bowed his head for a minute... After the moment of silence the voice continued,

"Due to this tremendous loss, we will give an amnesty to certain individuals. Please come to the office as your name is called."

This tragic moment of the country turned into a victorious moment for Peter. As soon as he heard his name on the release list he revived as a flower in the early spring, after two years and three months being on a death row. Energy and happiness filled every muscle of his body. Freedom! – What a beautiful and powerful word! Like a bird that escaped from an iron cage, Peter's soul was flying among the clouds in the high blue sky. He forgot about all these years of torture; all he wanted, was to be outside of the heavy fence of the camp.

The day has arrived when Peter walked out of the camp as a free person! He was heading toward the home of his childhood. Once again he looked at the place that was suppose to serve him as his home for the last three years. Some others, including his friend, weren't as lucky as him...

It was about time to look toward his future. There was a huge journey about six thousand miles ahead of him. He had to figure out how to cross this enormous distance without having any money in his pocket and without any mode of transportation in his hands. He was determined to get home safely no matter what! His first mission was to get out of Sakhalin Island and reach the coast of the continent. With the Lord's grace, Peter got a boat ride all the way to the coastline and this was his first successful achievement. Traveling on the ground was not an easy task either, but Peter had an internal fire that didn't give a place for disappointments. He persistently continued his way. He walked through deep forests, or if he was lucky, he would catch some truck rides. Sleeping under trees, trying to stay warm, and keeping something in his stomach, he slowly crossed "taiga" (dense forests between tundra and steppe). When he got to better populated places (villages, small towns), he would get a ride on anything that moves: horse carriages, tractors, country trucks, freight trains and so on. United by the sorrow and the losses of the war, people welcomed Peter and offered him food and shelter. He was touched by the kindness of the strangers and was really grateful to everyone who became a blessing along the way. He knew that God's hand was behind each and every blessing that he received.

Early spring was breaking the roads, the sun was melting mounds of snow. Most of the Russian roads were just dirt roads. Especially at this time of the year, all of the roads were muddy. Many times he had to help push vehicles out of muddy pits. Due to the road conditions and the distance to his home, it took him a few months until he saw the land of his childhood. When he finally arrived at that little village in the Western part of Belarus, his heart was beating so fast that he could hear the beats with his own ears. His house still looked the same way he left it. Nothing changed about it. The same fence around the property, the same barn behind the house. A bunch of chickens were running around, looking for some lost grains or may be a few worms for lunch. He slowly walked on the steps of his house... One knock on the door, another... He heard someone steps behind the door. The door opened, and he was looking in the face of the person dearest to him - his mother. "Mommy!" he managed to squeeze out of his throat, but had no chance to continue. His mother looked at him with shocking astonishment. The son that she never heard from in almost three years was standing on the steps and smiling at her! She was trying to hold on to the side of the door, but instead, she slowly passed

Journey Through Life

out on the floor. She couldn't handle the excitement of this unexpected appearance.

"Mommy! Mommy! It's me, Peter! Mommy! Wake up!" he was screaming. "Where is everybody? Please, help!"

His father came to see what was going on and couldn't believe his eyes. "Son!" His father squeezed him with all his strength. "Son, you are alive! And you are home!"

"Father, we will talk later, please get some water, mommy is unconscious."

Being refreshed and awakened with water, his mother opened her eyes. "Peter, my son! You are home! You are alive! I had been praying for you all these months and years! This is real, this is not a dream! This is a miracle! Thank you, Jesus!"

There was no end to the celebration and everyone praised God for His miraculous ways!

IV. Free from Stalin's camp, but not completely free yet…

After surviving "death" camp, the freedom seemed to be very sweet. However, it didn't last very long. The Communist system was always full of surprises and you never know what to expect from it tomorrow.

His friend Olga didn't have any communication with Peter for years but in her heart she knew that God would bring him back home safely. When he returned, it was a beautiful reunion of two loving hearts and they soon got married.

After the wedding they decided to make a great new start by leaving their small village, where both were from, and moving to a nearby town. Both of my parents' families were poor after the war; so my father and mother's inheritance was one big wooden storage bin with a blanket and one large piece of pork fat in it. That's all they had besides a pair of shoes and change of clothes for each. Carrying their belongings, they came out on the road, trying to catch a horse ride to town. A horse carriage stopped for them, they loaded their stuff and climbed on the carriage themselves. Olga was feeling really down. She was saying that she had no idea on how to make a living with just a few items that they got. On the contrary, Peter was very optimistic and cheerful. After long years of being locked up in the camp he couldn't stop enjoying the freedom. It didn't bother him at all that he had no possession. He was very positive that with God's help they would overcome all the obstacles in their way. His faith in God, his persistence and determination paid back, but meanwhile he had to continue walking on a "rocky road".

In less than in a year of living in freedom, he was convicted again without committing any crime. He didn't get a chance to recover from his first conviction yet! He just got married and started a brand new life! "Could these butchers leave him alone? What was the verdict?" The response to all his questions was simple – he still believed in God, and they counted that against him. He had to serve another capital punishment for them to clear the "religious smoke" out of his head.

Can you argue with socialist leaders? The answer is "NO!" Whatever they say – goes! The "Communist beasts" didn't drink enough of the blood of innocent people; they wanted more!

He was locked up for another two years and seven months (it was only half term); and then, by God's grace, he was considered "not guilty" and released.

After surviving another portion of the life of convict, some kinds of doubts were born in his mind. "Communism – the best political system in the world" didn't look that great to him. That was just a written statement to brainwash everybody! He couldn't trust them any more: what if they decide to lock him up for the rest of his life? Or, even worse could happen... It didn't look like the Russian authorities valued people's lives. Everywhere, where Communism was in power, people had no rights; and those who "thought differently" were always persecuted. Ever since that time, Peter was looking for ways to escape from the land, where millions of Christians poured out their blood and laid their bones in the ground.

V. Childhood in the Socialist camp

Starting from a very young childhood I understood that Christian people were not treated in the same way as everybody else. Christian ideas were quite different from communist ideas which caused disagreements, fights and persecution. Since elementary school, at the age of seven, I was forced to become an "Oktiabrionok", which was the first step on the way up the "Communist ladder". Every child in school was given a red star pin with a picture of Lenin on it, which represented the spirit of Lenin, the founder of the Communism. Growing up in a Christian family, I was a victim of the conflict between Christians and Communists. They always said, "Religion and God are incompatible. You have to choose between one or the other." Being raised by believers, I knew that Jesus was the only way and the truth. I wished that I had a power to explain it to others, but being just a little boat in the ocean of ungodliness, I had to keep this truth to myself.

Many times my schoolteachers and principal would pressure me to go along with the system. At the age of eight, I was defending myself in front of a mean and angry principal. One-day he called me to his office. With my little brain I was trying to figure out what that was all about. I was a very quiet and well-behaving girl in school, and also was an "A" student.

"What did I do wrong?" I was thinking to myself while walking to the principal's office. I opened the door and walked inside of the room. The face of the principal looked red, I could tell that he was upset with something.

"Sit down!" he commanded, his voice scared me a little.

Journey Through Life

"I don't like your attitude toward our school activities," he continued. "Why did you refuse to participate in our school choir? Did your parents tell you to do that?"

I was listening to his angry voice and trembled.

"I wish that I was a grown up like you, then I would tell you why," I was thinking, but instead I mumbled, "I cannot sing songs about Lenin, because I am a Christian."

After these words he exploded the "fire of anger", he couldn't control himself any more, "You are telling me that you, Baptist people, can do anything you want? Your lost-minded parents are using our Soviet motorcycles to drive to their mob meetings! Why do you have to listen to them at all? They are corrupting your future! Don't you understand? You will not be accepted in any good school or college or even get a fair job! Tell your stupid parents "Thank you" for ruining your life!"

His face turned burgundy-red, he forgot completely that I was only a little girl sitting in front of him. He was hitting the table with all his strength and screaming so loud that one of the teachers came in and took me out of the office.

All of the attempts to break my beliefs at the early years of my life never made me change my mind about being a Christian. On the contrary, they reinforced my belief in God. I was very thankful to God for taking a lead in my little life and His blessings never ended for me.

VI.   My Summer Adventures

When I turned fifteen I convinced my younger sister Dina to get a summer job with me at the collective farm. As many other students, we went to Lithuania, where we were hoping to make some money for our back-to-school supplies. We were employed as seasonal workers on a farm, pulling out weeds from the plantation of red beets. The work was very hard. We had to get up at six AM, chew on something and run to the field. At noon we would take a short lunch on the field to save time and then would continue weeding until midnight. Tired from bending in the field for a whole day and from walking a mile back home, we would fall in a deep but short sleep, which was never enough to restore our original energy. Six AM alarm would ringggggggggg… in our ears every single morning except Sunday. My hands were rough, full of scratches and cracks from the dirty work in the ground. They didn't look like tender hands of a young girl. The sun burned my face and body, but I never gave up.

One night my sister and I worked late, trying to finish one large weeding section on the field. It was getting very late, close to midnight, but we didn't want to stop. At the end of the field we straightened out our spines and looked around. There wasn't anybody around; we were all alone in the field; in the depth of the night. We looked up - the sky was all covered with stars. Everything was so quiet that we could hear the rustle of leaves and sometimes the voice of an owl.

We picked up our choppers and started to walk back toward the town. In the complete silence that was surrounding us we could hear our own breathing. We reached a little forest and were about to take a turn around it, but, suddenly, something jumped out of the forest and ran toward us. When the creature noticed us, it stopped and we recognized it as a wild pig (hog). Frightened by this sudden midnight meeting we stopped, rooted to the ground. I thought that my breathing stopped too. My heart heavily pounded in my chest. Before I realized the danger of the situation and figured out what to do next, the pig made a U-turn and ran back into the forest. I took a deep breath, grabbed my sister's hand and we ran and ran and ran… When we stopped to look back, we realized that there was no hunt behind us, and we finally slowed down. We jogged around the longer side of the forest, avoiding any other unpredicted forest adventures.

Soon the forest became thinner and we could see some houses behind the trees. I felt a release of tension and something similar to a smile appeared on my face. I looked at my sister Dina. "We almost out of the woods," she said and I knew at that point that she was all right. Soon we approached our apartment and praised God for His safety and protection. We knew that the guardian angel was with us that night.

VII. My First Election

Many times since I was very young I heard my father's discussions with the local authorities about the election process in the Soviet Union. "You just love to fool people," my father would say. "Do you know the meaning of the word "elect"? The definition for ELECT is "to choose, to select". You twisted this definition completely by writing one candidate name on the ballot and then asking people to "elect" that name. This makes no sense at all. Why do you want people to vote for someone that you had already appointed?" Nobody ever answered that question for him; they would just try to change the subject of the conversation or laugh in response. This was one of the "rights" that communists offered to people: "right to vote"... for one candidate. All the rights in the Soviet Union, such as right to vote, right to hold demonstration, right to choose a religion and hold worship meetings, freedom of speech, etc. were twisted to the point where they became nonsense. After all, the freedom was just on the paper; in real life it was a "red dictatorship".

When I turned eighteen years old, I was invited to participate in the local election. The election poles were established in the building of the High School. I was excited of getting new, grown-up responsibilities in my life. "Now I am eighteen," I was thinking, "I can think for myself and make my own decisions, I am not a minor any more! Greaaat!" With these kinds of thoughts I was getting ready for my first election.

It was early morning when I got out of the house heading in the direction of the High School. I was anxious to get there before anybody else. I had to be first at my first election. At the voting place I was given a ballot and was instructed to drop the ballot into the voting box. When I looked at the ballot, I only saw one imprinted candidate name. "My father was right," I said to myself. "This really doesn't make sense to vote for one candidate. How could it be called an election?" Anyway, I went to the voting box and stretched out my arm to drop the ballot, but someone grabbed my arm.

"Hold on, please, hold on," a person with glasses and a big camcorder in his hands was talking to me. "I am a reporter from the local newspaper. I need to make a picture of a person that votes for the first time. Is this your first time voting?"

"Yes," I said.

"How old are you?"

"I am eighteen."

"Great, you are everything I need! Please wait and I will let you know when to drop the ballot."

It was getting more exciting every moment! "Now my picture is going to be in the newspaper! I have a great beginning!"

After taking my picture, the reporter got my name, address and some other information. While he was still talking to me, someone from the local authorities interrupted our conversation and pulled him aside. After a few moments the reporter came back, he seemed to be a little troubled. "I am sorry," he said. "I cannot publish your picture in the newspaper, because you are Christian. Sorry!"

All the celebration and excitement that I had that morning immediately disappeared like the clouds. Disappointment and frustration were the only two things left in my heart. I was convinced one more time, that it was impossible to be a Christian and live well in the USSR.

VIII. New Year's Eve

As everybody else in the world, Russians have the same tradition of getting together for a New Year's Eve celebration. Very often such celebrations would go on the whole night until dawn. In nineteen hundred eighty my friends and I were invited for a New Year's Eve celebration in the town of Novoye, that was about a hundred miles away. Ten of us got together and made plans for the upcoming trip. We had to take a bus half way and then take another bus. At the end we had to walk for two miles to our final destination. We made all the necessary arrangements, got prepared well in advance and anxiously waited for the last day of the year to come.

Winters in Belarus were very cold with a lot of snow and low temperatures. Sometimes we had to dig tunnels in the snow to make walkways to the main roads. Weather forecasts were not accurate and most of the time weren't available at all. We had to deal with Mother Nature on a day-to-day basis. We were hoping for a favorable weather for our trip.

However, when we came to the bus station on the scheduled day, we were told that all the bus routes were cancelled due to a winter storm. This news disappointed us. We had to make some adjustments to keep everybody happy. The idea came up from one of us to walk to a train station and use a train instead of a bus. Being "young and restless", we were so determined to get to our destination that even the weather couldn't stop us. "Ready, set, go!" We went on with our new plans. In a few minutes we were already on our way toward the train station. It was just a mile away, but it took us longer that usual, because we were walking against a strong freezing wind that was blowing a lot of snow into our faces. The snow was getting heavier and the wind was picking up, it was slowly turning into a major snowstorm. Our hands and feet were frozen and we realized that we should have taken more warm clothes with us to keep our bodies warm. Despite of the extreme weather conditions, we persistently continued to walk forward, trying to make it to the train station. When we got there, we found out that our train was two hours late due to the severe storm. Instead of sitting inside and waiting for a train, or going back home, my sister and I decided to walk to my friend's house (her name was Liuba), who lived nearby. We wanted to borrow some scarves, hats, sweaters and other warm goods to help us get through the raging storm.

When we came outside, we could barely see anything. The swirls of snowflakes filled the whole atmosphere. A white blanket of snow was getting higher by the minute. We had no idea that this short task would be an extremely hard or otherwise impossible task. I guess there was no time for logical discussion, so we just walked stepping in each other's footprints. It was really difficult to pull out our feet from the deep snow. We looked like two snowmen, all covered with white flakes. Our noses were red from the freezing temperature. My boots were full of snow and my feet were wet and frozen. Half a block before we reached the house, the snow was so high that we couldn't walk any more, we had to crawl. Lucky us, the gate of their fenced property was open and without further obstacles we crawled on the top of the steps and knocked on the door. "Oh dear children, who let you out in this kind of weather?" Liuba's mom proclaimed when she opened the door and saw us completely frozen and covered with snow.

Liuba's mom was a very nice lady. She pulled us inside of the living room and placed us in front of the burning fireplace. Fire heated up our frozen parts and revived our strength. After drinking hot tea and picking up warm goods, we walked out of the house through the back door, where the snow was not as high. We got back to the station faster and easier.

At the station we divided the clothes between us, pulling on additional sweaters and pants and covering faces with warm scarves. We were "all set" to continue our travels.

Meanwhile, late train arrived and we happily got in. In about an hour we got to a station called Zhabinka. It wasn't our destination, but we had to come out and change the train there. One more train and we will get to Berioza, and a couple miles away was Novoe... There wasn't anyone to say, "Kids, are you out of your mind? Stop moving around, find shelter until the storm stops!" So, we pursued with our itinerary.

When we got inside of the train station, the operator announced that all the scheduled trains were cancelled due to the severe weather conditions. What? Did we get stuck somewhere; nowhere? We couldn't go forward and we couldn't go back! Although we tried not to panic, it wasn't a great feeling to be stuck in the middle of nowhere.

Have you ever happened to be stuck between cities, or between subway stations, or perhaps in the middle of a tall building in an elevator cage? I don't think that anyone would be that excited about it. We were in a similar situation. Praise God that at least that we didn't get stuck outside in the snow.

We had to deal with the poor conditions of the station. The building had very poor heat and we had to constantly move around to stay warm. It was getting late, about ten PM. We tried to settle and wondered if that's where we had to meet for New Year's Eve? All right, we were going to make the best of it!

Ten of us made a worship circle and we asked God to be with us in this unusual situation. One of my friends and I came out for a prayer. Everything outside was covered with snow and visibility was very low. We closed our eyes and prayed for God to come forward and give us a way out of that train station. God revealed to us the following vision: "Train

Journey Through Life

was moving without any railroad, it was simply crossing the snow covered plain." We got inside of the station and shared the vision with the group. No matter what it meant, we believed that God had a plan for us. We read the Bible and quietly sang songs.

There were a few other unlucky travelers trapped by the weather in the same train station. Some noticed us reading and singing and were curiously looking at us time after time. Around 11PM a young man approached our circle and asked if we were Christians. We said: "Yes." To our surprise, he didn't just walk away, but on a contrary, was trying to hold a conversation with us. "I am from a Christian family, but I am not a Christian myself," he said. We all amazingly looked at each other and then at him. "My parents and my sister went to the city of Brest to meet for the New Year Eve with other believers," he continued, "but I didn't want to join them. I was trying to take a train and celebrate it at my friends' place. As you can see, I am stuck here for the same reason as you are. The only difference between us is that this is my hometown and I can walk home any time I want. Perhaps, you would like to join me in my house for a New Year celebration." He questionably looked at us and continued, "I didn't tell you that I am a Militia Lieutenant, but please don't worry, my parents told me a lot about Jesus." We were listening to the man's words and couldn't believe our own ears that he was inviting us to his house. I started to understand God's revelation to us. He really had a plan for us that night. "Yes, sure," we said. "We are really grateful for the invitation! All right, everybody, lets go before the New Year catches up with us!" And we went... We were walking on the snow-covered ground, not seeing anything but the snow around us. One by one, stepping in each other's footprints, we were following our surprise stranger. We formed a live train that was crossing the field of the snow, just like in that vision. When we got to our rescuer's house, we had just enough time to kneel down in a prayer before the New Year kicked in. We praised God again and again for His wonderful deliverance.

Alex, our new friend, forgot about his strict militia policies and accompanied us in a nightly worship. He asked us a lot of questions and we helped him understand some of the Biblical principals. Right before dawn we had a little nap, but soon the morning sun woke us up. That morning was so bright that every snowflake was reflecting the sunlight. It looked like the whole city was covered with a white sparkling blanket. There wasn't even a sign of a storm, except for the beautiful layer of snow. After saying "Good-bye" to our new friend we went back to the train station. All the trains were back to their normal schedule. We successfully took the train that brought us back home.

When my parents heard that we met for the New Year with the Militia Lieutenant, they were first shocked, thinking that for some reason we got in trouble and spent the night at the Militia station. (It wasn't unusual for Christians to be held at the Militia Station at that time.) But then they heard our story and we praised God all together for His miraculous ways!

A few weeks later, I went back to college. I met with Alex's sister Liuda, who was a Christian already. Liuda told me she was really happy to know that her brother Alex bumped into us at the train station. God touched his heart and made him welcome us into his home. That's how we could testify to her brother and worship together with him. Later Liuda and I made good friends.

IX. Our Trip To Tallinn

Peter, a friend of mine, was serving in the Russian Army far away in Siberia. As I said earlier, serving in the Russian Army was a mandatory act for all boys who reached eighteen years old. Every male had to serve for two years. Everyone who would try to avoid it or escape it would be persecuted or imprisoned. Peter joined the army exactly at eighteen.

He was serving in the military unit located near one Siberian town. He was excited to discover a Christian church in that town. On his day off he managed to find his way to the church. In spite of the fact that the church didn't have many members, they had a decent group of youth that welcomed the soldier with a great hospitality. There he met with a beautiful girl, Anna, and fell in love with her. It was a mutual love. During his two-year service they got very close to each other and finally Peter decided to propose to Anna. She gladly accepted his proposal. Without losing any time, Peter and Anna got married right before Peter was dismissed from the army.

When Peter came back home, he brought a surprise with him. He introduced Anna to his parents as his wife. Peter's parents were really surprised, but when they got to know their daughter-in-law, they happened to like her. Everyone who knew Anna liked her. She was very sweet, passionate, sociable, moreover, she was very pretty. Everything seemed to be going fine for this new couple until I found out that Anna suffered from heart and kidney problems. She couldn't work hard or walk fast. Due to the kidney disease her legs would swell up after any minor walking around her house. There was nothing that the doctors could do to improve her conditions. With time her conditions got even worse.

At that very time some pastors from Finland used to come to Tallinn, Estonia, to hold church meetings and to pray for sick. It was a long-term revival that took place on the second and forth Saturday of every month. Everyone who heard of those miraculous events would travel from far away places to attend those prayer meetings.

Tallinn was on a distance of seven hundred miles away from my home. Since I already visited Tallinn few times, Peter and Anna came to me begging to bring them there. I didn't hesitate, because I knew that Anna needed a prayer for healing.

Soon we were on our way to Tallinn. The train was measuring mile after mile, flying like a bird, but on rails. We were sitting comfortably in a coupe wagon and watching how the sun was slowly moving down the horizon. The best way to travel was nighttime because time flies while you sleep. When we woke up in the morning, we found out that we arrived at a Lithuanian train station, where we had to change the train. Before too long we were sitting in a different train that was heading straight to Tallinn.

It was late autumn in my country. This time of the year the weather could be really chilly, even cold. At the time of our visit trees already lost their leaves and stood there with their dry and bare branches. Flocks of birds had already departed flying toward south. Everything was preparing for winter even though winter didn't arrive yet. While the train was running north, we could see through the window deeper and deeper fall panoramas. Temperatures were slowly falling down. A few pedestrians on the streets were covering themselves with long coats, warm scarves and hats hiding from the chilly autumn wind. "Look," I said to my companions. "There is a man running after his hat, blown away by the wind. It must be very windy outside." There was a young lady sitting on a bench of a train station, trying to wrap her little children in a warm blanket. I tried to imagine Mother Nature talking to people; it would probably sound like a strong wind, warning humans,"Beware, winter

Journey Through Life

is coming! Hey, get your warm wardrobe ready! How about your heaters? Have you had the service done on them?"

If I could color autumn in my coloring book, it would probably look mostly brown: sad brown leafless trees, brown bare ground, brown wooden bridges, houses, benches, etc. In the absence of sun, it felt like the sky and the clouds were brown too. Gloomy rainy weather took place of a beautiful sunny summer. All surrounding was melancholy, just like gloomy Eeyore from Winnie the Pooh.

Estonia was the most Northern Republic of my country. In July it could get seventy degrees Fahrenheit at the most. If you know the state of Florida well enough, you could compare Florida's winter with an Estonian summer.

The train was slowly pulling to the platform of Tallinn's main train station. The dreary strong wind burned our faces as soon as the door of the train opened. We came out of the wagon, studying the picture of Tallinn's fall. It was this windy snowless winter chill, that gets to you through the bottom of your sleeves, neckline and all the openings that it can find.

Due to her kidney disease, Anna had to use her husband's and my arms support to walk. We slowly walked her down the steps of the train and into the station. It was an early Saturday morning and the station was not functioning fully yet. A few early travelers were crossing a huge hall looking for a coffee machine or some light breakfast. Others were still catching naps on the benches of the station.

We sat down on one of the benches and started to discuss the strategies of the upcoming day. Anna's conditions worsened after the long traveling. Her legs were swollen so much that the zippers of her boots would only go up half way. She definitely needed to stay in a sitting or resting position. Although the train station didn't promise much for her, her husband Peter and I decided that she was not going to walk around, unless she absolutely had to. We both tried to create the best environment for her as much as we could. Peter and I took turns in making arrangements for that day. While Peter was taking care of the luggage and the breakfast for us, I was calling some friends for information about the church services. Not being able to reach anyone by phone, we had no choice but to go to the church ourselves and find out what the schedule of the services was.

The church was located really close to the station, just a few blocks away. We took a trolley, then walked a little and here it was... After all our efforts we were finally standing in front of the church. Anna was on her last breath, but her spirit went up when she saw the place where she wanted to be for so long. It's like she was going to meet with the president. She got new hope, believing that she will come out of this church a healthy person.

New disappointments were waiting for us when we got in the church. The church custodian greeted us and apologized because there were no services or prayer meetings that week. "Oh, dear! We didn't know that their schedule had changed! Wow! What do we do? We traveled all this way with a sick person just to go back empty-handed? Could Anna handle the way back with all this discouragement added to the problems that she already had?" This bad news put us emotionally down; it was like someone poured the bucket of freezing water on our heads. The custodian looked at our confused faces and probably felt sorry for us. "Please sit down", he said. "Let me make a few calls, may be I can do something for you." We speechlessly sat down. Each of us was thinking about something. I guess we were still trying to hold on to our hope. I was praying, "Jesus, please give us good news. You know that we came here with an outstanding need. Please be merciful to us."

After a little while the church custodian came back with an unusually shiny expression on his face. "You must really be God's children," he said while walking toward us. "That's

Journey Through Life

why He takes care of you. I found out that some other people besides you arrived from far away for the prayers. Due to this fact, the church committee decided to schedule an emergency prayer meeting in the small sanctuary of the church. But there is one thing that you have to do, which is to wait for two hours until everyone gets here." While I was listening to this announcement, I already started to thank God in my heart, " O, Jesus, thank You for Your grace and mercy! I knew that You wouldn't let us travel all this way just to go back home with broken hope! Thank You forever and ever! Amen!" We made ourselves comfortable on the soft benches and took a little nap.

After some time church members and visitors gathered in a small worship hall and the service began. The congregation sang a few gospel songs and the pastor opened the service with a prayer. Then a speaker came to the microphone.

"Good Afternoon, brothers and sisters," he said. "Are we all ready for God's miracles? I am sure that He has a miracle for everyone here, we just need to believe! Do we have enough faith?" He looked around the hall and continued…"I would like to share with you a beautiful story of one little girl, who believed in a miracle and therefore received what she was asking for. Her name was Sonya and she was only eight years old when she her heard Mom and Dad talking about her little brother Georgi. He was very sick and they had done everything they could afford to save his life. Only a very expensive surgery could help him now… and that was out of the financial question. She heard Daddy say with a whispering desperation, "Only a miracle can save him now."

Sonya went to her bedroom and pulled her piggybank from its hiding place in the closet. She shook all the change out on the floor and counted it carefully; three times. The total had to be exactly perfect. No chance here for mistakes.

Tying the coins up in a cold weather kerchief, she slipped out of the apartment and made her way to the corner drug store. She waited patiently for the pharmacist to give her attention, but he was too busy talking to another man to be bothered by an eight-year-old.

Sonya twisted her feet to make a scuffing noise. She cleared her throat. That did no good. Finally she took a quarter from its hiding place and banged it on the glass counter.

That got his attention!

"And what do you want?" the pharmacist asked in an annoyed tone of voice. "I'm talking to my brother."

"Well, I want to talk to you about my brother," Sonya answered back in the same annoyed tone. "He's sick... and I want to buy a miracle."

"I beg your pardon," said the pharmacist.

"My Daddy said only a miracle can save him now... So how much does a miracle cost?'

"We don't sell miracles here, little girl. I can't help you."

"I have the money to pay for it. Just tell me how much it costs."

The well-dressed man stooped down and asked, "What kind of miracle does your brother need?"

"I don't know," Sonya answered. A tear started down her cheek. "I just know he's really sick and Mommy says he needs an operation. But my parents can't pay for it... so I have my money."

"How much do you have?" asked the well-dressed man.

"A dollar and eleven cents," Sonya answered proudly. "And it's all the money I have in the world."

"Well, what a coincidence," smiled the well-dressed man. "A dollar and eleven cents... the exact price of a miracle to save a little brother."

Journey Through Life

He took her money in one hand and with the other hand he grasped her mitten and said, "Take me to where you live. I want to see your brother and meet your parents."

The well-dressed man was Doctor Kriuchkov, a well-known surgeon specializing in solving Georgi's malady. The operation was completed without charge, and it wasn't long until Georgi was home again and doing well. Mommy and Daddy were happily talking about the chain of events that had led them to this place. "That surgery," Mommy whispered. "It's like a miracle. I wonder how much it would have cost?"

Sonya smiled to herself. She knew exactly how much a miracle cost... one dollar and eleven cents... plus the faith of a little child.

Do we have the faith of a little child in us? That's all God needs from us to perform a miracle. He doesn't even need our dollar and eleven cents! Everyone who has this kind of faith please come forward!" The speaker finished his speech and looked around waiting for people to come forward.

The group of ministers gathered together in a circle on the platform and held their hands together in prayer. They were praying for Jesus to be in the midst of them. After the prayer one of the ministers came up to the congregation and asked everyone who was ill and would like to be healed to raise their hands. Although the worship hall was not filled as usual, I saw risen hands everywhere around me. Those who needed to be cured from their illnesses and go home free of pain lined up in the aisle. One by one they came up to the prayer circle and the ministers laid their hands on everyone's head. The ministers brought each sick, tired and hopeless person to Jesus with a strong prayer. I didn't know the problems that those people carried with them, neither did I know those people. All of the faces that I saw were new to me. I just heard their voices when they praised God as they walked back from the platform. I watched Anna move closer and closer to the platform. Then she walked up to the prayer circle. She walked slowly due to the pain in her swollen legs. Then she carefully walked up the steps. This picture was captured in my eyes and was saved in my "memory cell". I knew Anna's diagnosis and what she suffered with. My eyes never stopped following her, and I watched every move that she made. When she set her foot on the first step, one of the ushers gave her a hand and walked her up to the ministers. I saw her surrounded by them with their hands on her head. They closed their eyes and prayed for her. The prayer was so strong that I felt like I was connected to the prayer myself. When the prayer was finished, ministers made a way for Anna to go back to her seat. But Anna didn't go back; furthermore, she never stopped praying. In her desperate voice she was asking God for a miracle and praised Him at the same time. Her voice was getting stronger and stronger. After quite a while she stopped, opened her eyes and started to walk down back in the direction of her seat. I was looking at her and noticed that her walking speed increased. Wait a minute, where was she going? Anna didn't stop at her seat, she just passed by us like we weren't there! Then she started to run around the worship hall. "Anna," Peter and I were calling her with astonishment. "Anna, where are you going? We are here waiting for you!" But she never heard us, she kept running. She made about three circles around the church hall and finally came back to us. "Listen," her voice was very loud, she almost screamed! "I cannot sit on the bench any more, something makes me feel like I grew wings." Anna pulled us out of the building. When we finally stopped outside to ask her questions, she said that she felt some kind of lightness in her legs and her whole body! She looked down, so did we; her boots, zipped halfway were sliding down to her ankles! She pulled those zippers up, but her leg muscles seemed to shrink and the boots were hanging on her legs so loosely that I heard flip-

Journey Through Life

flap sound when she walked. She didn't walk normally any more, she ran from street to street. Peter and I were behind trying to catch up with her. She reminded me that Energizer rabbit that kept going and going and going… Where did she get that energy? Where did the leg swell go? Was that real or just a dream? I shook my head few times to make sure that I was awake. This was a reality!

The miracles are real if you believe that God is real! I realized once again that God is real and that He is All-powerful. He is the highest Power in the whole Universe! He is the only One who can answer your prayers! He Is Who He is and nobody can compete with Him, nor replace Him, nor reduce His power! He stays forever and ever!

We took a train back home. It was one of the most joyful returns I ever experienced in my life! This time I saw a miracle, a real miracle, with my own eyes! I felt like sharing this experience with everyone I met. I talked to people on the streets, train station and everywhere I went. I wanted people to hear a live testimony from my friends and me. I also want you, my dear reader, to believe in what you just read about. This is not fiction, but a very true story! May God bless you and help you find Him! Please invite Him into your heart!

X. My brother's childhood friend

My brother had a childhood friend Gena – they grew up on the same street. Gena was a very nice boy, easy to get along with. They shared the same hobbies and interests and were great pals. I remember when my brother was dragging an old bicycle from the dump with high expectations of converting it into a moped (similar to a motor scooter). Every day after school Peter and Gena would get together in our backyard and put their hands on dirty and rusty metal, trying to turn it into a running vehicle. After some time they finally succeeded…

One day I heard the roaring sound of a motor – the newest invention of two kids was put to the test. Sniffing, puffing and producing a lot of smoke, a new vehicle jumped out of our backyard, carrying Peter and Gena on the top. The two boys squeezed themselves in to fit on the bike seat together – both of them wanted to feel the excitement of running wheels at the same time. I was looking through the window and couldn't hold myself from a good laughter. I regret that I didn't take a camera to photograph such a funny and memorable moment in my brother's life.

A mechanical hobby was not the only hobby that the friends shared. They were raising chickens, rabbits, guinea pigs, hamsters, etc. They sure had a lot of fun together. There was something else going on behind this boyish fun; while having fun together my brother at his young age managed to share the Gospel with Gena. He started to do it way back from elementary school.

Gena came from a family of non-believers. His parents were a working class family. They never considered God or Christianity as an option. The problem with Russian people was the Communist influence. Christians were never honored, furthermore, they were always persecuted and considered to be a third class society. A majority wouldn't lose their government benefits for a religion.

Maybe out of respect to my brother or maybe for some other reasons, Gena never objected the religious subjects that my brother used to discuss with him. He was always a good listener. He quietly gathered all the words about Jesus that my brother told him and kept them in his heart. Being a minor (the youngest child in his family), Gena couldn't change his parents' lifestyle. At the same time he was my brother's best friend with his full devotion. If he told his mother about his discussions with Peter; perhaps, she wouldn't let him see his best friend anymore. Therefore, he kept it a secret.

Meanwhile, Gena's father separated with his mother and left them. Aunt Anna, Gena's mom, was raising two children of her own (Gena and his older sister Alla). The broken commitment between his parents put a shadow on his mind. Maybe then Gena realized even more that the Christian lifestyle was a better lifestyle, because Christians follow Biblical laws that teach the importance of family values.

Growing up with a single mother Gena was an obedient son and also a good student. Soon his mother became proud of the fruits of her labor – she had two well behaving and obedient children. She loved Gena even more for his devotion to her. She suggested that he should go to a military school after High School. Gena listened to his mom, he agreed that this wouldn't be such a bad idea. "I could make a good lieutenant or even a general," he thought, because military education was honored in Russia.

Military schools in Russia were very tough and demanding. Only selected individuals could be admitted. The admission requirements to military schools were set high: candidates had to be excellent in academics, physically fit, and have a strong mind. On top of everything, the candidates were not allowed to practice any religion. Gena met all of the requirements and was admitted into the school without any problems. Soon he became a proud marine, but even more proud was his mother. It was that unique pride of a mother for her son, who exceeded her expectations.

After the first year of school Gena came home for a summer vacation. Aunt Anna was very happy to see her lieutenant-to-be and made a welcome party for him. Gena looked completely grown up and his uniform made him look even more mature. She noticed that there was something different hiding behind this uniform, but she couldn't figure it out. Gena adjusted to a normal civilian life and relaxed in the comfortable home environment. It felt good to be home after the rough military lifestyle.

One day Gena decided to open his heart to his mom and cautiously approached her. "Mom," he said. "I love you very much and respect you with all my heart. Please listen to what I have to tell you. My conscience is telling me that I have to accept Jesus and become a Christian like Peter and his family. Peter was telling me about Jesus throughout my whole childhood and now I realize that this is the right thing for us to do. Jesus took all our sins and carried them to the cross with Him. He was crucified for our sins and became the Victim first, but then the Victor and the Savior. Mom, do you know that Jesus died on the cross and after three days was resurrected by His Father? He is alive! He took our sins to make us free from them! His blood was poured out from the cross and washed all of our transgressions, so we could be saved and could inherit eternal life! The only thing that we have to do is to give our hearts to Jesus and He will do the rest. I cannot become a Christian yet because the military regime will not let me, but I would like you to pray for me and I will come to Jesus at the right time. Mom, I beg you, please go to Peter's family and tell them that you want to become a Christian. They will tell you what to do. Please do this for me. Do you agree?"

Journey Through Life

Aunt Anna was shocked by her son's testimony. She didn't know what to think about it or how to respond to her darling and deeply loved son.

"Mommy, let me tell you a story that might help you with your decision," said Gena, when he noticed that silent confusion on his mother's face. "Please listen to me. There was a wealthy man who lived with his son. Both of them loved to collect rare works of art. They had everything in their collection, from Picasso to Raphael. They would often sit together and admire the great works of art. When a war broke out, the son went to war. He was very courageous and died in battle while rescuing another soldier. The father was notified and grieved deeply for his only son. About a month later, just before Christmas, there was a knock on the door. A young man stood at the door with a large package in his hands. He said, "Sir, you don't know me, but I am the soldier for whom your son gave his life. He saved many lives that day and he was carrying me to safety when a bullet struck him in the head and he died instantly. He often talked about you, and your love for art." The young man held out his package.

"I know this isn't much. I am not really a great artist, but I think your son would have wanted you to have this."

The father opened the package. It was a portrait of his son, painted by the young man. He stared in awe at the way the soldier had captured the personality of his son in the painting. The father was so drawn to the eyes that his own eyes welled up with tears. He thanked the young man and offered to pay him for the picture. "Oh, no sir, I could never repay what your son did for me. It's a gift."

The father hung the portrait over his mantle. Every time visitors came to his home he took them to see the portrait of his son before he showed them any of the other great works he had collected.

Galina Cherubin

The man died a few months later. There was to be a great auction of his paintings. Many influential people gathered, excited over seeing the great paintings and having an opportunity to purchase one for their collection. On the platform sat the painting of the son. The auctioneer pounded his gavel.

"We will start bidding with the picture of the son. Who will bid for this picture?" There was silence. Then a voice in the back of the room shouted,

"We want to see the famous paintings. Skip this one."

But the auctioneer persisted,

"Will someone bid for this painting? Who will start the bidding? $100? $200?" Another voice shouted angrily,

"We didn't come to see this painting... We came to see the Van Goghs, the Rembrandts. Get on with the real bids!" But still the auctioneer continued,

"The son! The son! Who'll take the son?" Finally, a voice came from the very back of the room. It was the longtime gardener of the man and his son.

"I'll give $10 for the painting." Being a poor man, it was all he could afford.

"We have $10, who will bid $20?"

"Give it to him for $10! Let's see the masters!"

"$10 is the bid, won't someone bid $20?"

The crowd was becoming angry. They didn't want the picture of the son. They wanted the more worthy investments for their collections. The auctioneer pounded the gavel. Going once, twice,

"SOLD for $10!"

A man sitting on the second raw shouted,

"Now let's get on with the collection!"

The auctioneer laid down his gavel,

"I am sorry, the auction is over."

"What about the paintings?"

Journey Through Life

"I am sorry. When I was called to conduct this auction, I was told of a secret stipulation in the will. I was not allowed to reveal that stipulation until this time. Only the painting of the son would be auctioned. Whoever bought that painting would inherit the entire estate, including the paintings. The man who took the son gets everything."

God gave His Son 2,000 years ago to die on a cruel cross. Much like the auctioneer, His message today is, "The Son, the Son, who will take the Son?" Because you see, whoever takes the Son gets everything."

Gena looked at his mother. He saw the tears rolling down her cheeks.

"What do you think about the story, Mommy?" He asked, because he knew that the story touched his mother's heart.

Gena went back to his school but his mother started to visit our church. May be she did it out of respect for her son or maybe because his words touched her heart, but she did. Soon she realized how truthful the words of her son were and accepted Jesus. She became a Christian and got an ongoing desire to learn more and more about the Bible. Day after day, week after week Aunt Anna was reading the Bible, growing in faith and constantly praying for her son. We were very happy to watch our new Christian neighbor and to see the changes in her life. She discovered new happiness and excitement in Jesus that she was never able to obtain anywhere else before. There was no comparison of her new discovery with anything else in the world. She found the real treasure, the real truth and the real meaning of life, furthermore, there was an eternal life. All the goals in her life changed; she started to pursue a righteous kind of living and her face was glowing out of love that filled her whole being completely.

Gena continued with his military career. On the third year of school he noticed that his excitement of becoming a military officer was fading away. The more he thought of it the less he desired to become someone who he only dreamed about in his childhood. "How come?" he was questioning himself. "My dream is about to come true, why doesn't it excite me any more? Did something change within me or maybe my dream was wrong?" He was searching for answers everywhere, but didn't get any luck. Instead of an answer he kept hearing Peter's words that were buzzing in his ears, "Gena, remember, that Encyclopedia doesn't have all the answers, but Jesus does. He will answer you when you ask." Gena read many books and searched Encyclopedia but it didn't do any good. He couldn't find out why his soul was so empty and what he needed to do to fill his heart with happiness. After struggling for a while, he decided to listen to his internal voice and presented his requests to Jesus in prayer. At the very same time his mother was praying for him in his hometown. Gena anxiously waited and hoped to hear a response from God, although, he didn't even know how God would communicate with him.

One day when he was getting a bus ride from school, his school-friend pointed at one of the buildings that they passed by and said,

"Do you know that this building belongs to a local protestant church? That's where all these uneducated believers get together and worship their God. Who would believe there are still some people out there who steal from themselves? They waste their lives, give up their happiness, leave all good things in life just for God to whom they pray every day!"

Gena listened to his friend and just said, "Oh, yeah?" He didn't have a response for his friend and kept quiet all the way to the dormitory. Gena walked out of the bus but his head was full with unanswered questions. "Did Jesus use my friend to point to me at this church? Could this possibly be an answer to my prayer? I am going to find out..." Full of thoughts, Gena walked into his dormitory room. He decided to visit this church the following weekend.

On Sunday he anxiously drove to that church. When he walked into the church and sat down on the bench, he recalled all the conversations with his friend Peter. Gena felt so comfortable listening to the words of the pastor, he felt like he had always been there. Maybe he belonged there? Everything that the pastor said started to actually make sense. He didn't notice how he started daydreaming. His memories brought him back to his childhood, to all the fun that he had with Peter. It sure was a memorable childhood...

The pastor's voice pulled him out of his thoughts. "My dear friends," the pastor was saying. "I would like to give you a sermon about one visitor. One day, a man went to visit a church. He arrived early, parked his car, and got out. Another car pulled up near him, and the driver told him, "I always park there. You took my place."

The visitor went inside for Sunday school, found an empty seat, and sat down. A young lady from the church approached him and stated, "That's my seat! You took my place!" The visitor was somewhat distressed by this rude welcome, but said nothing.

After Sunday school, the visitor went into the church sanctuary and sat down. Another member walked up to him and said, "That's where I always sit. You took my place!" The visitor was even more troubled by this treatment, but still said nothing.

Later, as the congregation was praying for Christ to dwell among them, the visitor stood, and his appearance began to change. Horrible scars became visible on his hands and on his sandaled feet. Someone from the congregation noticed him and called out, "What happened to you?"

The visitor replied, "I took your place."

Jesus Christ took your place on the cross for you, my dear friend. He made the salvation really simple for you, the only thing you need to do is to open your heart for Him. Bring Him into your life and He will make it eternal for you. This is the greatest gift that anyone could ever offer to you – to live forever in paradise with Jesus. Please don't deny this precious gift – choose LIFE!" Pastor stopped his speech and closely looked at the congregation. Then he continued, "My dear friend, if you are looking for an answer and cannot find it anywhere, please come forward and we will pray for you. Jesus is your answer!"

Gena looked back to see if there was someone else to whom pastor was talking... But then he realized that the "someone" was he. His blood went up to his temples and his body was shivering from the touch of a power unknown to him. He couldn't understand what was happening to him? Something pushed him up from the bench and he slowly walked to the podium. He kneeled down with the pastor and kept feeling the power flowing through his body. Something supernatural was happening to him, something beyond his understanding. He raised his voice in prayer and the words were coming out of his mouth without him talking. He felt like there was someone else inside of his body talking for him. Gena prayed, "Jesus, thank You for revealing yourself to me. Thank you for finding me in this big and cruel world. Jesus, I feel your love and your power! I am giving you my heart, my life and everything I have! Now I know that you are an answer to my prayers and to all my questions! You are the missing puzzle of my life! Thank you again and again for coming into my life!" Gena couldn't stop praying. The prayer was pouring out of his lips by itself. When he opened his eyes, he saw that he was surrounded by ministers that were praying with him. Everyone was thanking Jesus for the miracle that just happened in Gena's heart. He just experienced a new spiritual birth. He felt like

Journey Through Life

Jesus came down and touched his heart. It was a happy and joyful moment: he tasted a piece of heaven.

After this experience nothing mattered any more. All priorities in his life switched around. Jesus became his first priority; and where was Jesus; there was love, life and continuous joy!

When Gena went back to school, he didn't hide his conversion into Christianity, he couldn't hide it even if he wanted. It was written all over his face, "Gena is a Christian!"

The college authorities got the news about Gena's transformation. They called him to the main office right away. "There are some rumors are going around that you became a Christian," the general said. "Is that true?"

"Yes, it is," said Gena. "And I will never regret it."

"Are you out of your mind? How could YOU, such a bright student, make such a worthless decision? It's up to you; if you want to follow your God or your brilliant career, you have to choose now! As you know, you cannot advance in the college, unless you change your mind about God. You have three days to decide. If you decide to deny your silly ideas about God, you will be promoted to the higher military level. Otherwise, you will be denied higher education everywhere within the nation. Now go back to your room and think it over." Gena was quietly listening to the general's speech, but in his heart he had a firm decision: his life is with Jesus. This decision was permanent. Therefore, after three days he had to say "Good-bye" to something that used to be a treasure of his life: the career of his dream.

Inspired by events happening to him in the past few days, Gena was on his way to his homeland. Looking in the train window, Gena was in his deepest thoughts, thinking over and over about the new treasure that he found in Jesus. Peace and joy were filling his heart up to the top. He was imagining his upcoming meeting with his mother and all the happy news that he was going to share with her. He knew that God will never leave him, furthermore, God must have something better for him than the military career.

From what happened to Gena next, you would see that God really had a plan for him. Gena became a minister and accompanied by three other ministers, he went to the Far East of Russia to bring the Gospel where it was never heard before. Soon Gena became a pastor of the church that he built himself. The church was filled with newborn Christians brought to Jesus by Gena's ministry. "It doesn't matter how you begin, but what really counts is how you end," said one Christian Gospel pastor. It is really interesting to see how all things work for the better for those who trust God. My brother Peter was very excited about the spiritual growth of his friend. He just planted a seed but God raised a huge tree.

Dear reader, if you ever decide to trust God in your life, this decision would change your life dramatically. It doesn't matter who you are or what you are going through, God will make you a new person and will give you a new life. Just come to Him and you will never regret it! Amen!

XI. The Grechko Family

There were many friends in our lives as we crossed the years in Communist fields. We were good friends with the Grechko family. They had five children, just like our family. Each child was about same age as we were. They had the same goals as us – to defend Christian rights in the Soviet Union. We kept good communication with them, although they lived on a decent distance from us. No matter how you look at it, but they were our great and trusted friends.

One day they appeared on the steps of our house. O wow! We were so glad to see them! They sure were full of surprises. However, this time they looked kind of puzzled, and everyone was carrying a backpack. It felt like they had a really important business to take care of.

"Is everything all right?" my father and I approached them with the questions. "Oh, yeah…" Ivan's voice sounded unsure and then he added, "We would like to ask you for a prayer, maybe God has a message for us."

"Sure! All right, lets call everyone and make a prayer."

We prayed with them. After the prayer my father said, "I saw a vision. There was a road and a huge lion was lying on it. It was chained to a tree. The lion was blocking the way and no one could pass by safely. But then the lion fell asleep and at that moment it became possible to pass by that lion." We looked at our guests. They were smiling.

"We got our answer," they said. "Please let us take care of something very important, we'll be in touch." After a short conversation they picked up their backpacks and left our house.

I was trying to understand what was going on and why they didn't tell us anything as they used to? We were always open with them plus we were close friends. Whatever it was, it must be something important! They are in God's hands, when the time is right I will find out. And I was right.

One week later my mother turned on the radio and tuned it on BBC station. She used to listen to the world news. A BBC reporter was talking about the breaking news that just happened.

"One Russian family crossed Russian/Turkish border and they are in a custody of Turkish authorities." The story sounded interesting so my parents continued to listen. "These kind of things happen in Russia once in a hundred years. The family of seven people – elder parents and five grown up children – escaped from the Soviet Union on their feet. All seamed to be all right, besides some bruises, scratches and cuts on their hands. The family name is Grechko."

"What???" my mother screamed. "Children, please come and hear this! The Grechkos crossed the border to Turkey!" I couldn't believe my ears; I jumped and yelled "Wow! I knew something was going on! How did they do it? How did they cross the largest and toughest border in the world without being captured? How could that be possible?" And then we all understood the vision: "The lion fell asleep" – God answered their prayers and protected them from the danger. I wanted to know more details.

Later BBC interviewed the fugitives and I found out all the details that I wanted to know. My dear reader, you will not believe what happed to this family in their travels! It sounded just like a fairytale. Like in a fairytale it was a fight of good and evil and the "good" won all the battles, because "good" stands for God. Unlike a fairytale, the story was very real.

The Grechkos were planning an escape from the country for a while, but the time was never right for them. This idea was planted in their minds for years and one day it grew into a huge tree. They got the feeling that the time had come for them to take actions. To leave the country legally was out of the question, therefore, they planned to run. Due to the extreme risk of being captured, they didn't just execute their

Journey Through Life

decision. They prayed and fasted and looked for an answer from God. They decided to pursue their plans only if God gives them a positive response. Otherwise, they shall stop and look for other options. As I already said, that the vision with the lion cleared all their questions and reinforced their decision. They believed that God would put the lion to sleep for them to cross the border safely. They had no doubts any more and moved on with their plans. Due to high secrecy and the potential danger of being heard by the wrong ears, they couldn't share their future plans with us.

After leaving our house they took a train as far as they could get to the closest point of the Turkish border. When they reached their desired destination, they hid in the forest until dark. For a while they stared at the sun waiting for the huge fire circle to go down, but the heavenly monster of light didn't want to move. Time is our strict manager and if you don't go along with it, it could cause you a lot of frustration. If you are not patient at the times when you have to wait, or if you are not racing with it when you are in a hurry, you could loose a lot of nerves. Grechkos patience was tested at that critical moment of their lives. Although they wanted to go ahead as fast as they could, God had a perfect timing for every item on their schedule, no matter how nervous they were.

Soon it got dark. They lined up and moved on... The oldest brother, Ivan, was guiding everyone with a map and a compass in his hands. Six people followed Ivan. First they had to cross a wide field covered with smooth yellow sand – for about a mile. They walked very quietly; every noise could cost them life. When they finished crossing the sand field, they took a deep breath; everything around was still quiet. They couldn't waste any time. Even though they were extremely quiet stepping in each other footprints, they could still be easily discovered by the Russian border-guards. Their first task was accomplished successfully, but what to expect next? What will be their next challenge?

They walked into their next challenge soon; it was an electric fence. They slowly crawled to the fence, but then what? This was a dead end... The only thing that was left for them to do - to lie flat on the ground and pray. In addition, they heard a distant sound of a helicopter in the air, which was growing stronger. They started to see a strong projecting light that was getting closer and closer. Customs helicopter was doing his nightly routing inspection. Soon they noticed that the helicopter was not going away any more, it was making circles around them and stayed just above the spot where they laid. The Grechkos knew that they were spotted. "Oh, dear Jesus! If Russians put their claws on us, this would be the final chapter of our life!" They felt trapped between the powerful electric fence beside them and this scary helicopter on the top, but there was no way back. They knew how risky this operation was but they put themselves into God's hands. "Dear God," they were praying. "What could compete with your power? There is no power in the world that could beat the power of You, All-powerful God, who created Universe and angels, who created the earth, and everything and in it, including little people like us. The only thing you asked us to do was to believe in you and trust you and you would take care of the rest. You answered our prayers and gave us a revelation about that dangerous lion that was blocking our way. We are next to this lion right now. But then you said that the lion fell asleep. We believe that you will put this lion to sleep and will help us cross this border safely. We are putting everything in your hands, Lord! Amen!"

After the prayer they were just lying on the ground and waiting for a miracle. It was like in a story of Moses; but instead of being trapped between the Red Sea and the army of the pharaoh, they were trapped between electric fence and custom's helicopter. A chill was going through their bodies

Journey Through Life

and their hearts were pounding. It was very dark and windy. Confused and terrified, they laid on the ground for a quite some time, paralyzed with horror.

The sounds of thunder took them off their meditation. "A thunderstorm is coming?" They couldn't believe their own ears... In normal life we don't like thunderstorms. We usually hide until they are over. But for the Grechko family potential thunderstorm gave a gleam of hope. "What is going to happen next? Is God answering our prayers?" They anxiously waited to see what happens next. The thunder was getting louder and louder and finally they saw the first close flash of lightening. Big drops of rain fell to the ground. Very soon it was hard to see anything. They were getting soaked in huge streams of water. The lightning was hitting somewhere very near. Suddenly, they heard something like a huge explosion. They closed their eyes and ears and squeezed into a ball. When they opened their eyes, they saw a miracle. Actually, they couldn't see anything at all – it was an absolute darkness. What do we call a miracle? Something extraordinary, that cannot be explained otherwise. Miracle for Grechkos was an answer to their prayer. They couldn't see anything at all, because the lightening caused a power outage. The fence, yes, the fence had no power! The helicopter lost its way in the storm and disappeared! "Thank you, Jesus, for saving us! You are real! You came to save us as you saved the Israelites! You opened the Red Sea and removed the power from the fence! You put the lion to sleep! Thank you, thank you, thank you!"

They jumped to their feet. Ivan held a flashlight, Vladimir pulled out a small ax from his backpack (they were really prepared for everything) and made a hole in the fence. In a few minutes they were on the other side of the fence. They celebrated the victory over that monster fence, but in reality it was way too early to celebrate. The finish line was still far out of their reach.

What was hiding behind the fence? Was that the end of the borderline? Oh, no... Right behind the fence was a minefield. "God, where are You?" In a desperate hopelessness they were looking up in the sky again. Trying to understand what to do next, the father broke up in tears. Was this going to be his final moment with his family? He fell flat on the ground and burst out sobbing. Ivan saw that his father's emotions were crushing down and rushed to the rescue. "Daddy, daddy, please calm down. Jesus told us that He will protect us and He was with us all the way up to this point. We cannot lose hope now, please put yourself together, it's almost over." The father lifted his head and looked at his oldest son, who tried to calm him down. He thought for a minute and realized that Ivan was right. "All right, Ivan," he said. "I am glad that you have this faith. Probably, God wants you to lead us through this field. Go ahead, I will follow you."

Nothing could remove the power of mines, not even a thunderstorm. They couldn't do anything without a prayer. Prayer was their compass and protection at that crucial moment of their lives. They asked God to direct them and to show them the way. And He did! He never fails His promises! With some hesitation they started to walk on the minefield. Ivan was the first one and everybody walked behind him one-by-one. As soon as Ivan put his foot ahead, he heard the voice: "I am the way. Walk with Me." The voice was telling him where to put his foot and everybody behind him was stepping into his footsteps. After an hour they crossed the dangerous minefield safely! Then they realized they Jesus was walking in front of them invisibly and they stepped into His mine-protected steps. Hallelujah!

After a very little break the Grechkos continued to move ahead; the road lay through the mountains. They walked and walked and suddenly stopped, they reached the end of a cliff...What now? The only way to get to the other

Journey Through Life

side of the mountain was the hanging road. A suspension rope, which looked like a heavy metal cord, was connecting two mountains to give people a way to cross the canyon. But where was the wagon? There was no wagon. Probably nobody used this mountain road for decades. What to do? Is there a choice? Risk and danger were their brothers these days. They had to act and act fast before the Russians caught up with them...

"We have to cross over the canyon by hand," Ivan said. The tired fugitives had no choice but to go on. They put their pain aside and desperately continued their way. "Let's go!" Imagine seven people (including elder mother and father) hanging in the air, holding on to the rope with their bare hands. A deep canyon was under them and the tall dark sky with a few stars was above. Seven small figures were slowly moving with their hands on the rope, trying to reach the other side of the mountain. It would be really scary if they didn't believe in God. They believed in their hearts in protection from above. It was a very painful experience. Determination and the strength from God helped them to cross the canyon. Their hands were cut and bled. They cried from pain, but the song of praise and glory came out of Nina's mouth and everyone joined her. Crossing the canyon was the last step to their freedom. Russia was behind them and they were walking on Turkish land. God put the lion to sleep and gave them an escape from the communist camp. They were free from Russian's hunters, but what to expect from Turkish authorities?

They gave themselves up into custody of Turkish government. Turkish authorities investigated their case and confirmed that they really were Russian fugitives. They asked the family where would they like to go from there. Grechkos expressed their wish to go to Canada, where they had a brother and an uncle. This was the last test of their faith. Will the Turkish let them go to Canada, or will they give them back to Russians? They remembered that God was on their side and He will be until the end! In a few days the Grechkos were landing in a Canadian airport. Their brother welcomed them with his opened arms.

XII.   A Summer Job...

One summer I decided to get a seasonal job. I applied in a few places and didn't have to wait too long – there was a job opening for a GYM attendant in Children and Youth Sport School (CYSS) of the city. They called me for an interview and I was hired. I was excited that I could make some money for the next school season. To my surprise, the director of the school was someone from my neighborhood. Mr. Kolosov was also the former teacher of my military class (this was a mandatory class for all middle school students in my country). I smiled when I saw him at CYSS, but he didn't recognize me. All right, I didn't try to remind him who I was, I got busy with a new job.

Everything was going fine for me at the school until one day. There was a basketball game playoff and many basketball fans came to see it. Many of the visitors were high-class executives, VIP's, and government authorities. And guess what? One of the top government officials, Mr. Usovitch, recognized me. He knew my family and considered my parents as "untrustworthy Christians." Do you know why? Just because they didn't hide their faith, like many others did. We were different from many others, because we stood up for our beliefs. The authorities considered us as fearless and provocative, but dangerous elements of society. Actually, this was the prototype of real Christian in the eyes of the government.

I felt that Mr. Usovitch reported me to my GYM director, because Mr. Kolosov started to act strangely with me. My working hours were late evening hours. After everybody leaves I was suppose to straight everything out and lock the building. Usually I was the last person to leave the school. A lot of times I used the GYM's shower room right before I went home.

One night when I was finishing my shower and preparing to leave, I heard footsteps behind the door. Somebody knocked on the shower door and the voice asked who was there. I recognized the voice of one of the GYM teachers.

"It's me," I said. "I am almost done."

"What are you doing there at this hour?" he asked.

"What do you mean, what am I doing here? I am finishing my shower and preparing to go home." He went somewhere upstairs, meanwhile, I left the building.

I noticed that almost every other day there was someone visiting the GYM after the working hours. A few weeks later GYM director, Mr. Kolosov, called me to his office. I asked him if everything was all right? First he didn't respond, but then he said,

"There are talks in the city, that you carry a portable wireless radio set with you and use the GYM place after working hours to communicate with America."

I was looking at him and my eyes were getting bigger and bigger. "Are you all right?" I almost screamed. "What portable radio, what communication? Are you dreaming? Did you happen to find any of these devices in the school?"

"No," he said. "But if I ever find anything suspicious, you will be in a great deal of trouble. Besides, I heard that you bring some people with you to GYM. Is that true?"

"Well, my mother and my sisters came to pick me up from work few times. Shouldn't I let them get in?" I responded.

"Oh, no, that's all right. But remember my warning. I wouldn't like to find any evidence against you. All right? You can go now."

I was really shocked to discover that I am being watched. What did I do wrong? Was that a problem that I was a Christian and was defending my rights? Later I found out that just being a Christian you are automatically becoming an enemy of the Communist society. Christians

Journey Through Life

in my country were falsely accused in all kind of violations without committing any crime.

The director of GYM was really happy that I was only a seasonal worker. He didn't have to look for ways or reasons to fire me from the job. He just had to wait for a few more weeks. When my time was over I wished Good Luck to Mr. Kolosov. I knew that he would never hire me again.

This is one more story that tells you how rough it was to live in the Communist society.

XIII. Teens in the Army of Christ

Years passed by... Years of hard work and small pay. Years of raising five children on one little income, building underground church and battling with authorities. My father put all his strength and energy together to give the family his best.

In nineteen hundred seventy five Leonid Brezhnev (General Secretary of the Communist Party of the USSR) signed Helsinki agreement that any Russian citizen was free to choose a place to live in the world. Anybody could leave the country at any time or to come back to USSR. The agreement was never published or announced to the citizens. One day my father's friends shared the news with us regarding the agreement signed by Brezhnev. This was the beginning of a "new era"...

From the moment when my father found out about Helsinki agreement, the fight for freedom took a new turn even if it had to take eleven years to prove the existence of that document. Eleven years turned into a real fight for the Christians' rights: petitions, complaints, meetings, demonstrations of protest. It took a lot of courage, faith and physical strength to go through this complicated process that opened the road to FREEDOM!

"Immigrant group" (that's what everybody called us) was getting larger and larger. After nine years of constant activities, my father noticed that he was intensively followed by KGB agents and the events were taking a dangerous turn. Concerned of my father's well being and knowing that he was already convicted twice, I asked him to slow down. Then I thought that it would be much better and less suspicious to anyone if I continued my father's work. Who will bother to think that a young girl could hold such a serious responsibilities? It didn't take long for me to make a decision of taking a lead.

Journey Through Life

I knew almost everybody in the group and it didn't take me long to fit in. Although I was a new member of the group, I assumed my responsibilities immediately. I always made sure that I did the right thing, therefore, I prayed each and every time prior to starting any project. A few months before my involvement with the "immigrant group" I received a revelation from God. "God is going to give you a very interesting work. But it will not come on it's own, you have to look for it." This revelation came to my mind at that point and I understood that God talked to me about my involvement in the "immigration process". I started to make plans and work on the strategies. Where in the process I could contribute the maximum of my potentials? What do I do to help the whole system to work better? My first proposal to the team was that I going to make a trip to Moscow and try to meet with the president of my country – Konstantin Chernenko. By the looks on people's faces I understood that they approved my first proposal, although they were very surprised. The team's approval wasn't enough for me, I looked for God's approval. We all kneeled down and prayed. I received another revelation in a form of a vision. A tall mountain was covered with ice all around. Nobody could possibly climb it. There were two proposed choices in order to get to the top of the mountain:
1. To wait until spring time for the sun to melt the ice, or
2. To start breaking the ice and make the way up.

The vision was very clear to me. The mountain represented high government that nobody could reach. Waiting for the spring meant waiting for the government to change their laws and give Christians their freedoms. Breaking the ice meant starting to take actions on our own in order to enforce changes in the country. My choice was to start breaking the ice!

Galina Cherubin

It was summer of nineteen hundred eighty six, when I took my younger sister Dina to Moscow with me. In the beautiful city Moscow, the heart of Russia, we decided to start from the highest government of the country. Since the Communist Party of the Soviet Union (CPSU) was the only party in USSR, the General Secretary of the Communist Party held the main leading role. Konstantin Chernenko was the acting president of the Soviet Union at that time and we made a decision to get as close to meeting with him as we could. We tried asking for an appointment with President Chernenko, but we were denied any possibilities of meeting with him. The Central Committee of the CPSU office was telling us that the President does not solve the kind of problems that we had and we were referred to another high leading organ – the Supreme Soviet of the USSR. Getting nowhere in the other government office, we were referred to the third leading organ, which was the Ministry of Foreign Affairs, then to the Passport Office and then back to the Central Committee of the CPSU. Going around the highest government offices for almost a week, we were not able to obtain any answers from anyone, neither were we able to get an appointment with the president. Being pin-balled from one place to the other and back to the first place again, I was really disappointed with how we were treated.

At the end of the week, I approached the secretary of the Central Committee of the CPSU office with some questions:

"How many circles do we need to make around the Russian government just to get a logic answer to a simple question? Who is handling the immigration affairs? Why couldn't we discuss these issues with the President?"

She looked at me seriously and said, "I am sorry, but I cannot help you with your request. I can give you some advice: what you could do is to write a petition to the President, stating your problems and requests. Bring

Journey Through Life

it to me when you are done and I will send it to the proper department."

It wasn't the matter of choice, it was the only thing that we were able to do. We submitted a petition and returned back home (we lived about six hundred miles away from Moscow). We didn't even know that President Chernenko was very sick at that time.

XIV. Friends in the Soviet Army

During our trip to Moscow we decided to visit two friends of ours (we used to say brothers in Christ), who served their duties in the Soviet Army nearby. The army base was located about fifty miles away from Moscow. We took a bus and hit the road! The bus couldn't bring us all the way to the base, so we got out a few miles before and looked for a ride. Finding a ride was not a difficult task at all. "Beep..." we heard a signal behind us – it was a military truck passing by. Dina and I just managed to raise our hands just in time. The driver noticed us and we were on the way to the base. The truck brought us to a fenced area with the guardhouse next to a wired gate. Inside of the gate we saw a little city made out of wooden sheds – they were military barracks. After signing in at the guardhouse, a soldier walked us to one of the barracks, where our friends resided. The barrack looked really large, but felt cold and uncomfortable. The rooms had a few hard beds and nightstands. All the beds were covered with rough wool blankets of brownish/greenish color. Heat was really poor, soldiers had to stay with their jackets on to keep warm. The barrack had one bathroom with few toilets and few sinks in it. There was no need to make a ladies room, because there were no female soldiers.

When Valera and Kolia heard of us coming they were very excited. Smiling from ear to ear they walked into the visitors' room and gave us their generous soldiers hugs.

"Guys, you look so mature since the last time I saw you!" I said. "So how is everything going in the military life?"

Conversation started very fast, we had a lot to share with them. A lot had happened in their absence! The visitors' room was filling up slowly. Being long away from civilians or maybe simply out of curiosity soldiers were coming one by one and soon we had a crowd of twenty to thirty people. Dina and I brought some treats and while eating snacks,

Journey Through Life

we used that opportunity of friendly spirit to share the Good News with the soldiers. Somebody brought a guitar. Valera and Kolia were good musicians and soon we created a quick four-people band. We used to sing together before they went to the Army. It is true that music is a powerful tool to find ways to hearts. After we sang few songs, soldiers started to open up; they came up with questions about God, Jesus Christ and an eternal life. Our voices were getting louder and louder. After an hour the cold and uncomfortable barrack turned into a warm and friendly chatting room. The only thing that was missing - a fireplace, but there was no need for a fireplace any more. Instead of the fireplace there was a presence of the Holy Spirit and we could feel it. We prayed that the seed of the Gospel could grow in the soldiers' hearts.

Time was running out for the soldiers to return back to their barracks, "dead hour" was approaching. A "Dead hour" was the military term when all the activities should stop and everybody had to be in bed. After taking a few pictures and saying "Good night" the soldiers were unwillingly leaving the room one by one. Dina and I were brought to one small barrack room with two beds in it to stay overnight. We were trying to get some sleep, but the excitement of that evening didn't let us fall asleep fast. In my mind I was going over the events of that night and praised God. I thanked Jesus for giving us this opportunity to tell people about God. I wished that those young soldiers took it seriously. May be one day they could find Him. With these thoughts I fell asleep...

Heavy sounds of marching boots woke us up... It sounded like hundreds heavy tanks were rolling on the ground and echo was responding to it, "Uka! Uka! Uka!" "What is going on? Where are we?" Dina and I jumped out of the beds and looked in the window. Tens and maybe hundreds of soldiers were on their first morning practice. It was six AM. "Oh, yeah! This is a normal army day," I said. It was time for us to get dressed and go back to Moscow.

XV.   Sunday Morning Vision

Several days after our trip to Moscow I woke up on Sunday morning from a very exciting dream. It was so real that I felt a tingling sensation in my toes. My blood was running in the veins just like after running a race. Was that a dream or did I really travel in my sleep? It was difficult to tell. The only thing I knew that all of the events were photographed and kept in one of my memory cells.

I was back in Moscow with my sister Dina (the dream seamed to be very real). We went to the highest government office and asked for a meeting with the president and were treated with proper respect.

"Please sit down, I will call your names shortly," professionally dressed secretary pointed at the chairs in the waiting room.

We settled in two comfortable chairs and started to observe the life of the highest office of the country. I was looking in the window and watching the parking lot. I saw many government cars coming and going back and forth to and from the Central Committee office. I saw some men of the high authority of the country crossing the parking lot and discussing something while they were walking. I finally spotted a very tall person among others who was wearing white knee high boots. When I looked at the person's face closer, as close as I could look through the window, I recognized President Chernenko. Trying not to lose the president out of my sight (there was a lot of traffic on the parking lot), I focused my eyes on his white boots. I followed the boots for a while, until, to my disappointment, they disappeared from my sight. I finally turned my head away from the window, thinking of what might happen next.

After a while a man walked into the lobby and called our names. Dina and I got up from the chairs and followed him. In his office I finally looked at the person who wanted

Journey Through Life

to speak with us. He was not the president. The man was shorter than President Chernenko, the front of his head was bold and there was a dark spot on the bold area. He acted like a powerful man and spoke with authority. I was wondering who the person was?

"Girls", he said, "I am here to help you. What problem brought you all the way here?"

"Sir", I said, "we couldn't find a solution to our problem anywhere else, so may be you could help us. We are seeking a free immigration from our country. This was documented and signed by President Brezhnev in Helsinki in nineteen seventy-five. Sir, could you do anything to help us break through?"

"All right", he responded. "I will do it for you, but you have to follow my instructions. Go home and start preparing for your immigration: sell your house, prepare luggage and when you are done, come back to me and I will approve your Visa. Then you could leave the country at any time you decide to." We carefully listened to him and when he finished, he shook our hands Good-bye and we left. Out of the excitement of this unusual meeting, my sister and I jumped out of the office and ran toward the sunny outdoors, inhaling that aromatic air, that we didn't get chance to enjoy before. I breathed and breathed pulling fresh air deeply into my lungs. One more breath… and I woke up with all that excitement that I had in my dream. I knew immediately that God wanted to tell me something.

Three months after my night vision President Chernenko died, and Michael Gorbachev came to power. I looked at the first posted portrait of our new president and my heart stopped beating for a moment, because I already met with him in my dream: he was shorter than President Chernenko with the bold front of the head and the dark spot on it. I knew that President Gorbachev was the one who would open the heavy gate of the Communism, and he did.

XVI. Meeting with the Diplomats and Consul

It took more than weeks, more than months, even more than a decade for us to see the breaking of the iron curtain. Meanwhile, the battle for freedom continued...

One day Edward, Sveta, and Victor came over with very interesting news. "Guess what," they told me. "We got an invitation to visit American embassy. Would you like to come along?"

"Sure I would!" I quickly ran to the closet and pulled my travel necessities. With the same quick motions I changed into a jogging suit, grabbed the purse and before too long we were all sitting in a train that was heading in the direction of Moscow.

"Thank you for thinking of me!" I thanked my friends. "Do you have an invitation for me? Anyway, how does it work?" I was really curious about the mystery of this trip, because it wasn't easy for a regular Russian to get invited to the American embassy.

"Don't worry," Sveta told me. "It will work as well as a clock. Each of us got an invitation ticket and according to it each of us could bring one friend with them."

"All right, understood," I said. "Thanks again."

We were sitting in a wagon and counting the trees and electric poles through the window. It was a long journey. It took us fifteen hours to get to the heart of my country. Traveling at night seemed to be quicker. We woke up in the morning when our train was pulling to the belarussian station of Moscow.

Moscow is a huge city of ten million residents and close to one million guests every day. If you look down from a helicopter, you will see hundreds and thousands of people walking on the streets, crossing squares and boulevards,

Journey Through Life

and catching bus and trains. What a busy city! If you don't want to be lost, you just have to stay really close to your companions.

After taking a few subway trains we got to our destination. After a few blocks of footwork and here it was, around the corner – American Embassy. For a little while we were watching the gate from the opposite corner of the street. Four militia officers and two dogs were guarding the entrance, which was already secured with a heavy metal gate. The best security was well provided for the diplomats and the consul, simple civilians would never be able to get in. The watchmen with dogs walked slowly and confidently back and forth – you would never be able to break their hearts, this is for sure!

At last, here they were, our American friends Kathy, Margo and Michael. We ran across the street toward them.

"Wait! Wait! Wait! Where are you going?" The guards were catching up with us and blocking us from entering the gate. "Your identifications, please!"

"Oh, yeah! Sorry! How are you doing? We were invited here by Kathy, Margo and Michael," we pointed in the direction of the diplomats that were standing nearby.

"Is that true?" Officer turned his head toward the diplomats. "Were you expecting these fellows?"

"Sure, they are our guests today, that's why we came to the gate to meet them."

The officers checked our passports and invitations and let us through the gate. A passport in Russia serves as a primary identification form just like Driver License in the US. Our main goal of meeting with Americans was to brainstorm our problems, troubles and to search for the best solutions together. The diplomats were trying to help us the best they could. This Russian-American union played a significant role in a process of breaking through the Communism. One fact was for sure – the KGB was trying to prevent these kinds of meetings, but they couldn't keep up with us many times. It was because God's wisdom and power was always stronger than any of their dirty tricks. The only thing they could do with us was to write all the names on the "black sheep list" and try to catch us later. We met with diplomats almost every month. Even though, KGB agents followed us everywhere, we knew that such meetings were very important and necessary in "winning the war."

XVII. Boris

There were people that put their lives in jeopardy for the sake of others. The Bible says, "The greatest love a person can show is to lay down his life for his friends" John 15:13. Boris was one of the first ones who started to build the road to Christian freedom. He had to do it with his unbelievable will and efforts, even with the price of shedding his blood. He didn't care if he would survive that fight, he only saw the victory ahead of him, whether he survives it or not. Every Christian who was involved in that war between Christianity and Communism knew Boris, because he was always ahead of us. He took the hardest hit of the KGB but he never bowed in front of them. The only one that he worshipped was God. I always admired his courage and strength. I was very disturbed when I heard that he was arrested. Then I found out what he went through it was simply hard to imagine...

"Don't you see how powerful our system is, we will soon take over the world and it's all because we worship the devil instead of any old-fashioned God that you, stupid Christians, still follow. When will your weak brains get it? I wish that we push this "Christian" ideology out of your heads soon, otherwise, if you continue to be stubborn, we will mix your leftover bones with the mud of wild pigs and nobody would ever know what happened to you!"

This was the speech of someone who represented the most intelligent organ of the Soviet Union – KGB. He carried the highest rank of KGB power – general! Who could raise the voice against him? A simple citizen would never dare to get on the way of one of these.

"However, what's wrong with some of you, Christians," he continued. "Why do you act like you are not afraid? You are actually big cowards! It's probably just a matter of time and all of you will crawl to my feet. You just have to feel some of my new techniques!" The general produced some kind of smirk on his face. "All right, Boris," he continued his speech to one listener whom they captured on the streets and arrested for anti-Soviet politics. When the general paused, Boris looked in his eyes. He looked and sounded just like Satan himself.

"Who are you?" Boris asked.

"I am general Izumov, an investigator of "most wanted" cases. "Have you heard of Alexander Ginsburg and Baptist Pastor George Vins? They were exchanged for two Russian spies Anger and Cherniaev."

Boris heard a lot about Izumov - an experienced wolf of KGB, very popular with his "state-of-the-art" soul-breaking methods. Boris noticed that Izumov was looking at him with his drilling look, trying to read his mind. Izumov also knew that Boris was a tough bird. KGB had several attempts of "dilating" him, but none of the methods worked so far. A few times he came dry out of the water and smoke free out of the fire.

"Well-well, we will find out who has more power," Izumov paused and then continued, "Boris, we are not asking you to do anything hard. Just give us some information about your brothers-in-Christ. For example, we really need to know who initiated the complaint about the persecution of Christians in the Soviet Union? You should know that all of these are lies, nobody persecutes you, guys, when you follow our rules. We don't like when these kinds of documents come out of the limits of our country. Nobody needs to know our internal politics. Do you understand? NOBODY! But you, Boris, could help us a lot in solving these kinds of puzzles. You must be aware of what I am talking about. So, are you ready to give me names?"

"Names? I don't know what are you talking about? I wrote all the complains myself, that's all I have to say." Boris stopped talking and looked in the window where a few curious sunrays played with their own reflection in

Journey Through Life

the mirror. "How beautiful was God's creation from the beginning," he thought. "And how much corruption the devil brought to God's design after being cast out of heaven. Evil is trying to make as much destruction on the Earth, as it possibly could. It's very sad to see how the devil gets in many people's hearts and minds, making them do the ugliest crimes, that the human mind could ever design. This devoted KGB general doesn't even know whom he serves. He seemed to be proud of his skills and experience of breaking such hard nuts as I am. But he has no idea, that God backs me up and gives me strength to go through anything KGB would ever invent." "Boris," his line of thoughts was cut off by the loud voice of Izumov. "I didn't bring you here to make a fool out of me! Are you going to talk or not? Otherwise, I will make you talk! Guards," he yelled with the note of anger in his voice. "Come and take this stupid guy. I don't think he knows the price of not cooperating with me! Bring him to the "klopovnik"!" With these words two muscular guys jumped in the room, turned Boris's hands behind his back and pulled him out of the office.

"Hey, guys, we've got a fresh resident for you. Move, move, we need to squeeze him into the cell." They pushed Boris inside the cell of about six by nine-feet. Although, there were already fifteen prisoners, they pushed him in, making him number sixteen. Everybody was sitting on a cement floor, nobody cared about climbing on the wooden shelves, attached to the wall, that served as beds. First he thought that nobody climbed up because there were only four shelves and there was no way that all of them could fit there.

One of the convicts decided to climb up on a bunk and get some rest. After five minutes with the flood of profane words the convict jumped off the shelf, shaking something off his clothes and cursing the whole world. Hundreds of bed bugs were falling off his body. Russians call such bugs "klop". These type of insects live in beds, sofas, couches, everywhere they could find humans because they drain human blood with their sharp proboscis. Boris looked at the walls and was shocked from what he saw. He realized that the pattern on the uneven concrete walls was formed out of thousands of "klops". KGB used "klops" as one of the correction weapons for the most stubborn convicts. Therefore, they called that cell "klopovnik". Something turned inside of Boris's chest, then he closed his eyes and silently prayed, "Jesus, why did you send me to this awful place? I don't know if I could go through these trials by myself. But I am asking you to give me strength and wisdom, so your name may be glorified through my pain and suffering." Nobody could hear the words of his prayer; they could only see slight movements of his lips. Boris opened his eyes and realized that nobody cared of anybody else, but himself. Even if somebody was looking at him, it was just the meaningless look, like they were looking through glass. Qualities like kindness, understanding, and love were numbed in this horrible place. The only thought that every prisoner could have was probably, "how to remain alive in the jaws of merciless dragon".

Heat and thick smell of the uncovered toilet was making Boris sick. His head was spinning and he couldn't squat down any longer. He turned to a guy that was sitting next to him and asked if there was a possibility of getting some water. The guy looked at him with rounded eyes, "You must be new here. Don't you realize where you are? Don't you know what happens if you express your dissatisfaction here? "The dogs" will drag you out of here and will bruise you from your head to toe."

"The dogs? How could the dogs bruise me?" Boris asked, expressing his perplexity.

"Ha-ha-ha! He is new and doesn't understand anything! Not even our language! Hey, brothers, let's show our new

Journey Through Life

guy how he could get the water!" A moment later every convict in the cell jumped on the feet and after few seconds everyone was hitting the doors, walls, and floor and yelling for water! Boris shook his head; the noise was cutting his ears. In a minute few muscled guards with thick wooden rods appeared in a slot that was called "feeding window".

"Shut up! What are you yelling about?"

"We need water, we are drying up here!"

"Water? What else do you need? Maybe fried pork? Nobody called you to come here! You managed your way here, than manage your way out! No water for three days! If you make more noise, you'll get a "special treatment". Most of the convicts were already familiar with the "special treatment". However, some of them weren't. They continued to yell for water until mad guards dragged them out of the cell and started to hit their bodies everywhere they could reach. Soon everything became quiet. After the discipline action a few of those rebellious guys were dragged back into the cell and pushed inside, one was in the unconscious state. Three guys were bruised and covered with blood but still conscious, the forth one was unconscious. Boris went to him and tried to revive him by shaking his shoulders, but everyone else didn't seem to care.

"Just leave him alone, he will get back. This is not the first time." The prison community seemed to be ruled by animal laws: the strong lives, the weak dies. The day was coming to an end, but nothing changed in the surrounding environment. The smelly hot air was making Boris drowsy, his mouth dried completely without water, the annoying bugs were attacking him moment after moment. It was less than a day since he got here, but it seemed like an eternity. Boris started to count down the hours of stay in the "hospitality" of klopovnik. His legs were getting numb from squatting down in one spot, his head was spinning. He couldn't imagine staying here much longer.

"Jesus, please don't leave me in this awful spot," he was praying over and over. "Jesus, I know that you took heavy cross and went to die for us without any guilt. You experienced suffering, mockery and death and you told us to carry our crosses. I know that I cannot bypass my portion of suffering, but please give me strength to go through it. Please reinforce my physical strength and give me thankful heart for your name to be glorified in every breath that I make." Praying and thinking about greatness of God, Boris forgot about everything that bothered him at that moment. He felt like a spring of water was pouring through his arteries, refreshing and reviving him. Soon he forgot about his hunger and thirst and fell into the memories.

He remembered that worry-free time that he spent with his family on the sea while they visited his mother-in-law. How clean and refreshing was the water and he splashed it as much as he could. His wife was collecting beautiful seashells. "Boris, look at this one," she stuck one to his ears. "Wow, this is a real treasure!" he said listening to the sounds of the sea that was coming from the shell. He missed his wife and his six children, but he knew that God would not leave them even in his absence. His youngest daughter was only two-month-old, he almost didn't remember her, but one day he will meet her and will give her a huge father's squeeze!

Boris was awakened from his thoughts by the noise that he heard behind the door. He turned his head when the door opened and another poor soul was pushed in. "New resident" looked lost, his eyes were roaming around the room like searching for the place to land. He finally stopped his confused look on one of the bunks. He quickly moved toward the upper bunk and placed his few belongings there. Then he called the guard and asked for a needle and threads. The "New resident" climbed on the shelf and settled there. Boris was wondering how long would it take for him until he jumps down shaking off the bugs, but for some reason

Journey Through Life

he stayed there longer than Boris expected. Boris looked up trying to see what was he doing there, but when he looked up he was horrified. The "New resident" stitched his lips together and the bloody ends of the thread were hanging on both sides of his lips. Boris understood that the guy was probably threatened to admit some guilt that he wasn't responsible for. Evidently, the guy lost his mind. "Help! Help! Someone here needs an immediate help!" Boris was yelling in his full strength. "The dogs" arrived on the call for help and took the guy out of the cell.

Boris couldn't calm down that night. He was trying to close his eyes, but the visions of the hopeless face with stitched mouth never left him. How long was he going to deal with horrors of human cruelty? He didn't know. But one thing he knew for sure that God would never leave him and one day he would come out as a VICTOR, the VICTOR of Christ! Boris started to think of how to approach the lost and desperate scum of society with the news of Christ. It was a difficult task to get to the hearts of those that had nothing to lose. Do they have hearts or maybe all they have left was just a pumping blood muscle? Boris decided to brake the ice and started a conversation.

"Brothers," he said. "Why don't we tell each other some stories, the time will go faster and tension will be released." Two guys looked at him with some kind of surprise,

"Are you all right? What is that you wanted to hear from us? The story of how "the dogs" will brake off your last kidney tomorrow? Or maybe about how many of us will be carried out with our feet forward? Stories? Guys, he wanted to hear stories? We are not your mothers to tell you stories! If you knew that you wouldn't handle that, why did you get here at all? Why don't you tell us what brought you here? Were there some smart transaction of black market involved? Or perhaps, you sent one of the poor souls to the other world? Tell us, we are listening!" "Sure, I will tell you, guys, but it's not what you are thinking. I am here, because I am a believer of Christ."

The gang didn't expect to hear this response and one of them replied,

"This is all nonsense! Do you expect us to believe that?"

"It's up to you whether you want to believe or not, but that's what I am here for." Everyone became silent; they probably started to believe that Boris was telling the truth. Meanwhile, Boris used this moment of confusion and started to talk about Jesus. He told them how Jesus was born in a stable with animals, he told them about all the hardship of his life on the Earth and His crucifixion. "He was crucified for our sins because He loved us, although, He never committed any sin, He was pure like a lamb." There was a very deep silence in the cell only Boris's voice sounded with strong assurance. He was going on and on trying to deliver the word of truth to the hearts of the lost souls.

Three days later Boris was transferred out of "klopovnik" to a regular cell and never saw any of those guys again, but he heard that two of them accepted Christ in their hearts.

Mad KGB officers tried everything to break Boris's will, but he appeared to be unbreakable. Strong will and faith in God kept him from atheist corrosion. He had been tortured in the "cup cells" that looked like the storage lockers made in the size of a human being. "Cup cells" were aluminum lined closed rooms 3x3 feet square, 7.5 feet high. Every wall was covered with nails, which sharp ends were coming out from inside of the walls. The room was completely dark. The only position person could take there without being hurt was standing straight up. Boris was thrown in the "cups" at least twice a week, where he had to spend hours in a standing position. Many times he almost passed out. Under all the KGB "treatments" he never complained, but thanked God for being with him at those difficult times.

The newest innovation for tough political convicts was a "beauty treatment". Actually it was a simple solution made out of equal parts of chlorine, kerosene, acetone and one other secret ingredient. The solution was made to use all over prisoners' bodies, which caused excruciating pain and sometimes would bring poor victims into a shock. The pain would be so extreme, that many would pass out. The stronger ones would run around the large prison area, jumping and yelling endeavor to get rid of the burning body pain. This was an awful sight, but for some human beings (KGB officers, prison authorities) it was an entertaining event. They would watch those nude and skinny dancing convicts with distorted from the pain faces and would laugh very hard. It was a favorite free entertainment of cruel blood-sucking KGB (Kill & Go Barbarians). They called that event "dancing event". After the 30-minute of the "beauty" treatment, the prisoners would be pushed into a large shower room, where scoffing guards would play "catch the water" game with them. They knew that exhausted from the pain victims would do anything to get to a sprinkle of water. Therefore, they would open few shower sprinkles in the very corner of the room. As soon as barely conscious victims run to the corner tripping on each other, they would close those sprinkles and open them some place else, making poor human-like figures run around as a swarm of bees. When they would finally get satisfied with the conclusion of the evening "performance" they would open the whole shower. After the "beauty treatment" skin would peel off completely and it would take some time to heal.

After I learned what Boris went through I couldn't forget it. These were a few more awful details that I've learned about the country where I grew up. It was a horribly perverted system of humanity, where the beast had his full authority of damaging everything that was on his way. The good news is that God limits the beast authority because of the prayers of Christians.

I picked up the phone and called him. "Boris, I know what you went through, your story is a powerful eye-opener."

"You think so?" he asked. "I am glad to hear some positive responses. Many told me that I looked for troubles myself, that's why I got it so hard."

"I bet, these were the people that never did anything on their own, but just took a ride on someone else. If you didn't start it, it would be difficult for us, like my father and me, to continue the fight. You are the pioneer, you are my hero and if you didn't initiate the fight, the system would probably never break. We live in this world for the purpose of fighting with evil and winning souls for God. You did nobler job than many others that I met in my life. Thank you, Boris." He thanked me for my encouraging feedback and we finished our conversation.

Only a few could survive this KGB soul-breaking school, and Boris was one of the lucky ones. Being a bullet in a gun of authorities he wouldn't get burn. Being a shield, able to stand for Christian freedom in one of the most evil Communist countries, he got hit himself, but found strength to win the most evil war. Soon after his release from jail, the iron curtain broke in half and many refugees found their way to freedom. One stood for the rights of all – everyone celebrated the victory. Although, Boris would never receive any heroic recognition, like Martin Luther King did, he will always be recognized by God and by the few appreciative Christians.

XVIII.   Wandering in the Woods

Tamara, one of my friends, was always in the front row when it came to defend the freedom. She was captured by KGB on one of the immigrants meetings and was falsely accused of leading the anti-Communist movement. She was confined to one remote village of Lithuania. The area of her permitted residence was reduced to a circle of two miles radius, one step anywhere outside of this radius and she would be arrested.

Knowing of Tamara's situation, I was looking for an opportunity to visit her although she was awfully far from the place I lived. I couldn't find peace in my heart until I made a permanent decision of visiting her, because I knew how much she needed my support.

Dina and I were sitting in a night express train that was bringing us to Lithuanian border. We got out in the capital of Lithuania Vilnius. Since I couldn't read a Lithuanian map, I asked for directions to that small village Ladzinishkius. I was instructed that there was no bus that would bring us to Ladzinishkius. There was a bus that goes in that direction, but it wouldn't reach the village, we would have to walk for two and a half miles. It was ten PM when we were standing in the middle of the station and making decision. We decided to go. When the bus stopped, we asked the bus driver to show us the direction of where Ladzinishkius was. He looked at us with a surprise,

"Girls, are you sure, you want to do that? It's close to midnight!"

"It's all right", we said. "Just please show us where to go."

"O.K.! If you are so persistent, take that road and after two-three miles you will be right there." He pointed at a small route that was running through the forest. We thanked the bus driver and walked out of the bus.

It was a cold and silent dark autumn night. We could see neither stars nor the other heavenly bodies in the cloudy sky. We just stuck to the road that we had to follow. The road went into a forest and it got even darker. Walking through deep trees, we had no idea where we were. This small country road had no pavement; it was just a dirt road full of mud. Due to the darkness we couldn't see the time on my watch, we didn't know how long we walked already and how much longer we had to walk. I remembered the verse of the Bible,

"Doing good don't be dejected", so we kept walking, telling each other jokes. "Dina," I said. "Solve the puzzle. What vehicle moves without engine, doesn't need fuel and doesn't even need high beams?"

"Hmm..." Dina's search engine was running around the convolutions of her brain.

"Come on, come on," I said impatiently. "Are you giving up?"

"All right," she said. "Zero matches found in my brain. I give up." I was glad that she didn't resolve my puzzle.

"It's us!" I yelled in response. "Can't you see? No engine, no fuel, not even a flashlight, but we keep moving!"

"Ha-ha-ha..." she laughed. "Only you can come up with something extraordinary like this!"

"Good, I won! Now give me your puzzle..." Conversation (especially the humorous one) shortened our way and uplifted spirit. We didn't even know that there were a lot of deer and wild pigs in that forest, but God was watching over us. The forest was already behind us and the moon showed up from behind the clouds. It became much brighter. Few times we saw the road signs that were at the height of my stretched arm. I would lift Dina up and ask her to read it for me. The signs had navy-blue background and were very hard to read. They were also written in Lithuanian language...Dina did

Journey Through Life

a great job in trying to read those signs, because soon she read, "Ladzinishkius".

"Great! We did it!" I couldn't hold my emotions inside of me any more. "Hallelujah! We found the village! Praise God!" After walking through the darkness where our hearts were wrung with fear, we finally got the hope that it was almost over. We turned in the direction of the village, but how do we find the house, it was another gridlock...

According to our friend's description, the house was located at the beginning of the village, close by the main road (houses were not numbered in that remote village). We got to the closest house, but couldn't get to the steps, because there was a lot of water sitting around the house.

"O, yeah!" I said. "It rains a lot in Lithuania. Lets walk around and see where can we cross over this pond to get to the house." I slowly started to walk toward the house but WOW! I put my foot down and it went deeply into watery mud.

"O, my! Dina, watch out! My boots are full of water and mud."

I helped her to cross over to the steps. We walked up the steps with dirty and muddy feet. "I hope, that this is the right house," I said and started to knock on the door. Everything was quiet. I knocked again and again and then knocked on the window. Not even a sound in response! Then I looked around and saw another door. O. K. this was a twin house and probably nobody lived in the first part. We started to knock on the other door and soon we heard the steps. Someone turned on the light and opened the door... It was Tamara.

"Girls, dear, what are you doing here at this time?" she asked. "It's two AM! Come in please and take out your wet shoes, let me make a tea for you!" She was glad to see us and was really touched by our visit. We had a warm fellowship and then went to sleep.

The house was cold, the whole night we were trying to warm up under the blankets. In the morning we met with her little children two and a half-year-old boy and six months old baby girl. Children were wearing triple sweaters, hats and "valenki" (felt boots) to keep warm. Tamara was complaining about her hardships, especially in the winter season with children. She said that it was hard to keep the house warm due to the lack of insulation and poor heating system. "Everyone always goes to sleep warm dressed," she said. We brought some goods, which she needed and after spending some more time with them we were back on our way. We praised God for protecting us during this mission.

That was one of the things that we used to do to support other Christians, especially those who fell into disgrace of government and were under house arrest.

XIX. Maria Phedorovna – A Prayer in the Kitchen

Some of the activities that we used to do were meetings with Jews in Moscow. I was invited to one of the meetings once and was very excited about it. It was another trip that I had to make but I was ready for it. Prayer before travels was a standard procedure that we followed – "Don't leave the house without prayer." Another thing that I liked to do was taking my younger sister with me for a companion. We knew that prayers were protecting us as a shield from any kind of danger. We needed a guardian angel to lead us in our ways and to repulse the enemy arrows.

One of our guardian angels was Maria Phedorovna, a wonderful elderly lady with a golden heart. Her last name was Golden, which completely reflected her sweet personality. She would always welcome me in her little apartment in Moscow and would give me the best hospitality at no charge.

When Dina and I arrived in Moscow, Maria Phedorovna squeezed us with her special golden hug and we knew immediately that she missed us. That day she had more visitors than just us. There was a prayer meeting in her little apartment that very same day. After a few hours of fellowship, Dina and I got up – we had to be in time for the meeting with our group at the train station. Unexpectedly, one of the church visitors called me to the kitchen and asked me for a personal prayer. I expressed my apology trying to refuse it, because I was running out of time. If we were late the group would not wait for us and leave. Then all the efforts of this trip would be for nothing. But the lady didn't want to let me go.

"Please," she said. "It will be just a few minutes. I have an urge to pray with you." "All right," I agreed. "Just for a few minutes, that's all I have." After a short prayer Dina and I rushed to the door, we had to catch up with the time that we missed. I was hoping that we didn't have to wait for a bus for too long. Actually, we needed to take two buses and a subway to get to the place of meeting. Things didn't work exactly the way I expected. We spent fifteen minutes waiting for the first bus, then another few minutes waiting for the other... When we finally reached the station where we had to meet, nobody was there. I looked at the clock and saw that we were ten minutes late. Ten minutes! The time that we spent in prayer in the kitchen!

We spent all this time and money and didn't achieve anything? My soul was empty, I was disappointed and discouraged that we were left behind. We prayed for this trip, but why did it turn out this way? I couldn't understand it. "O.K. I blew it," I said to myself. We had no other choice but to leave Moscow.

At home I shared my disappointments with my parents. "Nothing happens without the reason," said my mother. "All things work together for our good if we love God. Romans 8:28." "All right," I said and walked away, trying to disturb myself from the memory of that disappointing trip.

The same evening my parents were listening to the BBC station, the only station that gave actual world news up to date. You could never get this kind of news from the Russian TV or radio station. While listening to the news, my parents heard that there was some kind of conflict that happened in Moscow the day before. BBC was talking about a huge meeting of Jews and Christians in Moscow, which had a bizarre ending due to KGB capturing and holding in custody all the attendees. My mother called me to listen to that. When I heard what happened in Moscow, I realized that God protected us from being captured, because we prayed. Only then I understood the purpose of that ten-minute prayer in the kitchen. God sent a person to hold me in the house for an extra ten minutes, ten minutes that made a significant difference for my sister and me that day. God kept me ten minutes away from danger. Isn't God great? He foresees our future, we just have to trust Him in all aspects of our lives. Things that seem to be bad turn out for good for everyone who trust Him and follow His ways! Amen!

XX.   Demonstration of Protest

Years of dictatorship were building up a pressure in the hearts of Russian people. Some of them were saying: "It cannot continue this way, it has to stop one day! We have to let the world know how much suffering Russian people (especially Christians) get through. Many tears dropped out of the eyes of thousands, and the rivers of blood of innocent people were poured on the ground! The day of freedom shall come, bright rays of sun shall shine in every dark corner, every shadow shall disappear and every crime of the cruel government shall be revealed to the eyes of the world. The cages of people's souls shall open and they shall raise their wings and fly like eagles towards the freedom that they dreamed about for many-many years. And the Earth shall celebrate the greatest delivery of the nation: delivery from miseries, delivery from suffering, delivery from tortures of the government's cruel regime, built by Stalin."

Do you know what the name Stalin means? It means steel, hard, tough, unbreakable. Those were characteristics of his regime – to push hard, to be tough, to kill in order to build the unbreakable Communist system by any price! Stalin was a very tough and jealous person, who didn't trust anyone, not even his own mother. He killed everyone, of whom he was suspicious; he also killed his own mother. Stalin's daughter – Svetlana - ran away from the kingdom of the cruel king, (her own father).

Many believed that the day shall come for the cruel leadership to open the gate of the Communism and lived by their hopes. Christians believed in better days, meanwhile, the fight for freedom continued...

A Christian group met in Moscow strategizing the future steps of Christian movement. I attended that meeting. The leaders said, "We need to remind our government that besides the "robots", (those who were brainwashed and blinded by the Communist theory completely) there are still people that think for themselves". The suggestion was made to call one of the largest demonstrations of protest in the country, which was supposed to involve people from different regions. The idea passed a majority of votes and the time and the place of the demonstration was scheduled. The demonstration was supposed to take place on one of the squares of Moscow. We tried to keep it a secret from the government and KGB. However, due to the hundreds of people involved in this event, the secret found a tiny leak and got into the ears of the authorities.

The day of the demonstration was approaching closer and closer. I tried to avoid any possible resistance of the local authorities. My flexible working schedule allowed me to take a train to Moscow three days prior to the event. Being very careful about this "risky business", I changed my traditional route that I used to take to Moscow. Instead of going west and then northeast, I went through the capital of Belarus, Minsk, which was located north from my city.

The train was entering the Moscow suburbs. I felt some kind of relief. Bill (my companion) and I looked at each other, speechlessly saying, "We made it so far, thank you, Jesus!" The train slowly pulled to the platform. Pushing the last cloud of smoke out of its funnel, it stopped by a huge building that carried thousands of people every day. It was a famous belarussian train station of Moscow. The train attendant announced the final train stop and asked everyone to get ready to leave. It was a late morning hour and the sun was moving close to the middle of the sky. It was brightening every corner of the city. The shadows were getting smaller and smaller until they almost disappeared. We could enjoy the view of this busy city. Pedestrians were crowding on the sidewalks and the crosswalks. The cars, trains and trolleys were trying to make their way through the busy areas of the Russian capital. Subway trains were on their full schedule moving thousands of Russians and tourists from all over the world from station to station. Subway stations, like beautiful galleries, were competing with each other by their unique mosaics and gold framed paintings. The look of each underground station would tell you a story of ancient Rosh (old Russia). If you've never been to the heart of Russia, imagine yourself "tinker bell" flying through one of the beautiful fairy kingdom. That's how nice and attractive Moscow was.

After a successful arrival in the capital I called my home to see if everything was all right there. My apprehensions about KGB were right. My father told me that he was under a house arrest. A few hours after I left my house, a KGB car pulled toward our house. The agents were watching every move that was happening in and around the house. My father told me that he was stuck and wouldn't be able to go to Moscow.

"Well," I said. "At least Bill and I made it. We will do our best to make the demonstration happen." I knew that we were a target of the KGB and was as careful as I could to proceed with our goal.

First of all, we had to arrange our stay. Our guardian angel Maria Fedorovna welcomed us in her little apartment, located close to downtown of Moscow. As I said earlier, she always had a place for us for as long as we needed one. As her desired guests, we would get the best piece of her attention. Praise God for giving us this sweet and caring friend in Moscow.

During the three days Bill and I were preparing for the event. We stored the banners, which we carried along from home, in one of the lockers of a belarussian train station. Then we called our American friends in the embassy. They promised to come and support us during the demonstration.

Journey Through Life

That day we went to the train station where we had to meet with brothers and sisters arriving from different cities. Due to the conspiracy this task was one of the hardest ones. We hoped that the KGB wouldn't recognize us. I was almost sure that we would get through unnoticed. Finding a needle in a haystack would be easier than recognizing someone in such a crowd of thousands of people. That's how busy the plaza was.

Suddenly, someone grabbed my arm, as I crossed the plaza. When I turned, I was looking into the face of a stranger. I asked him to let my arm go, but instead, he pulled out his identification. Trying to release my arm from this unpleasant stranger, I looked at his card - he was a KGB officer. Oh no! This cannot be happening to me! How could I be so wrong! How could I forget that the KGB had such strong and powerful multi-forces in my country. Their secret spider web was widely stretched over the nation. They would probably pull you out from the bottom of the ocean if needed.

"Sir," I said. "What is your problem? Why are you are stopping me? I was just crossing the plaza!" My voice had a note of frustration in it. Instead of answering me he said,

"Madam, may I see your ID please?"

A few steps away another officer also dressed as a civilian was questioning Bill.

"Things do not always go the way you plan," I thought. "What we were afraid of just happened to us. But God is in control of everything and He will turn everything for better." Since we realized that we were caught, we had no choice but to wait and see what's next.

Officers took a few minutes to review my ID and then asked me to follow them to the closest militia station. Nobody explained to me what I had done wrong, they simply brought me to the station. I was still fighting to prove that I shouldn't have been arrested, since I had no criminal evidence on me.

The only answer I got in response was that I had to catch the evening train and leave Moscow. I was told that no one owes me any explanations. "If you don't want anything to get uglier, just follow the instructions that we will give you and try not to walk away from these two fellows." "Two fellows? I didn't ask for company! Can you just let me go?" "Oh, no. You have to play by our rules, it's just can't be the other way."

Our "security guards" followed us everywhere; they even escorted us to the restroom. We could not detach ourselves from this involuntarily supervision for the whole day. We had no way to get to the place of demonstration. We just had to bear with our powerful "babysitters".

This was no secret to me that authorities tied my hands for the time of the demonstration. Legally, we had all rights on our side, because Russian constitution states: "Every Russian citizen has freedom of speech, freedom of religion, freedom of holding demonstrations and so on..." However, there were actual unwritten laws that people had to follow. Behind the scenes, Communists, along with the KGB spies, watched everybody, especially Christians, and dictated their own "constitution". In different words, Communism is a system of dictatorship, covered under friendly mask of hypocrisy. Same as Saddam Hussein, Fidel Castro, Taliban and other systems full of lies.

The day was passing by slowly. My head was full of thoughts of the events of that day. "What a mess!" I was thinking. "All these preparations were done for nothing." I hoped that other participants of demonstration had better luck than Bill and I. I also hoped that somebody made it. I was glad that the authorities didn't have access to my thoughts, otherwise, I could probably be found guilty in conspiracy to the demonstration. It looked like my friend Bill was deeply thinking himself, but the presence of the "babysitters" wouldn't allow us to communicate.

Journey Through Life

The evening clouds were moving in slowly and soon the stars came up in the sky. Our train was scheduled for the late evening hour and the time was approaching slowly to board the train. The station operator announced the arrival of the train and we went to the gate, preparing for boarding. Our guards followed us all the way inside the train. The train moved but we noticed that they remained in the train. "Oh, no! Are they going to follow us all the way home?" Once in a while I could see one of them passing by our compartment, spying on us. I felt very exhausted from everything that happened that day, therefore, I fell asleep without counting any sheep.

A ray of the sun sneaked in the window of my compartment and woke me up. WOW! The night passed by very fast! We must be close to the Belarussian City Brest! I jumped out of the bunk and looked at the time. We were close to the south border of Belarus. After a quick breakfast we gathered our belongings and prepared for the arrival in Brest.

One sharp idea came into my head. I whispered a few words in Bill's ears and he said, "All right." A few minutes before the train stopped we moved to the next wagon. When we looked back, we noticed that nobody followed us. Did we really lose our "tails"? They probably didn't expect any tricks from us by now. As soon as the train stopped, we jumped out and ran to the other side of the station. Being very familiar with that place, we crossed the plaza in a matter of seconds and in a few minutes we were sitting in our local train, that was bringing us to our homes.

The disappointment with that trip was not as dramatic, since I found some satisfaction in being able to escape from the "super smart guards".

Upon my arrival at home, my father shared his house arrest experience. The watchmen were there for three days and only left right before my arrival. I was happy again to be reunited with my family in our small and comfortable home.

This looks like a happy ending of the story, but guess what, the story didn't end yet. That very evening I went to sleep early. My body needed to recover from this emotional trip. As soon as I closed my eyes, I heard a knock in my bedroom door. "Who is this?" I asked and before I got to do anything, the door opened and I saw my mother accompanied by the local militia officer. "I am sorry," he said. "I was sent here to check if you were home."

"What did I do to you guys, that you are so suspicious of me?" I asked.

He didn't say anything except, "I am sorry" once again. I knew the real reason of that night visit. It was because the authorities lost track of me when I was changing the train, they were still afraid that I would go back to Moscow.

One day later, the city prosecutor called me to his office. What do you think he wanted from me? Actually, he wanted to find out what I was up to.

"Is there anything that you would like to tell me about your trip to Moscow?" he asked.

"How do you know that I went to Moscow?" I replied.

"Well," he said. "We have our ways."

"If you have your ways to know about people's business, why are you asking me this question? Use your channels to find out."

He looked at me, studying my face.

"Galina," he said. "Please don't take any further actions. Please give me a chance to take care of your immigration issues. Believe me, I am trying to be your friend." I knew that this was a wolf in a sheepskin, and I had to beware of these kinds of friends, but said nothing. After all, the Moscow trip wasn't a complete failure. We showed the authorities that we were not playing jokes but were really serious in what we were doing. They got the message, praise the Lord. This action was just another step forward to our goal.

XXI. The Trip to Brest

At the beginning of nineteen hundred eighty eight, under new administration of Michael Gorbachev we finally got an invitation from the United States. This invitation was everything that the Russian government required from everyone who wanted to exit the country. It gave us a stimulus to go on. This should be easier now! They just have to let us go this time!

There were two other Christian families that received invitations at the same time with us. We got together and went to the Passport Department. As I said before, nothing was easy in the Communist System. We were not surprised that our request was denied. This time they needed proof of the relations to the inviting party. We were told a completely different story this time. It was shocking, but it's true! This time we were required to have a relative in the US who could sponsor us. The denial from our local office didn't stop us from going further and we proceeded immediately. If the local authorities were causing problems on their own trying to mess us up we would find out about it. Or maybe they were just jealous of us. We went to the state capital, where we didn't get any good news either. Our request was denied in the same way as it was in the local office. In moments like this, I mean, the moments of desperation, I usually talk to God. Yes, I am not kidding, I talk to God in a prayer. That day I felt so helpless that I almost cried, "O, Jesus, please don't let me lose my last hope! Didn't you tell us to ask for anything in your name and it will be given to us? Didn't you already tell us that you would let us leave this country? I know that our day will come, but it feels like we are just fighting with the air without getting anywhere further!" I prayed and looked for some encouragement but there was a heavy stone on top of my chest.

"Galina, are you daydreaming?" my friend touched my shoulder. "Why don't we brainstorm the situation all together? Any ideas what to do next?" After a little discussion the group came up with an idea to write a petition and to fax it to the President Gorbachev's office?

"All right, we have nothing to loose; let's try this!" Everybody agreed and we went to the local Telegraph office. Fax service was fairly new at that time and we could only access it through the Telegraph office. They called it photo-telegram. We stopped in the closest Telegraph office and asked for a photo-telegram form. In a few words we composed our complaint to the President Michael Gorbachev asking him to unlock our gridlock. We got fourteen signatures under the petition and submitted it to the clerical window. I saw how the clerk's face turned white when she looked at the petition. Then she looked at us with a huge surprise in her eyes and said, "I need to speak with my supervisor." "All right, we will wait." We were looking at the clock... Five minutes passed, ten... It had to be an important subject to discuss, since she took all these time. Fifteen minutes... sixteen...seventeen... I was impatiently rubbing my fingers. "Where did you go, lady? We need an answer from you..." My thoughts were probably a little too loud, because the lady finally appeared in the window. "I need everyone's ID," she said. She examined our passports carefully, comparing the pictures with our actual faces. She was looking at us like we were some kind of terrorist gang. Then we paid for the service and our document was FINALLY accepted. Folding the receipt in my hands and smiling to the rest of the team, I walked out of the building. At this moment the pressure evaporated off my chest and deeply in my heart I was praising God for the answered prayer. I got a feeling that breakthrough was on the way.

We left the state capital with the uplifted hopes. On our way back we celebrated a moment of victory, although the battle wasn't quite won yet. We were chatting, singing and praising God, we didn't even notice how three hours of journey passed by and we were driving on the streets of our hometown.

My father and I came out of the vehicle and went toward our house. I picked up the mail from our old mailbox, painted in an unattractive brown color that was attached to the same brown wooden gate.

"Daddy, there is a card from the local Passport Department."

"Let me see," my father said. At a glance he looked at the card and turn toward our fellow travelers.

"Guys, don't leave yet, we have an invitation to the Passport Department."

At the Passport Department we were told that our request was granted to us and we should start processing the documents immediately. We couldn't believe our ears! Just this morning we received denial from the same people. Did Michael Gorbachev give them an order? How could this happen that fast? It was a miracle. God is never late if we believe in Him, it's always good to trust Him.

XXII. A Surprise Good-bye Party

It's wonderful to have a lot of friends! One wise man wrote awhile ago, "There is no need to have a hundred dollar bill if you have a hundred friends." This is very true if you have real friends, not just people that smile in your face.

Our friends got together and made a good-bye party for us. It was a happy and sad moment at the same time. It was one of these bittersweet moments of your life. The **Happy** side explains the part that we were granted permission to leave the country - it took us eleven years to achieve this goal. Finally, there was a breakthrough! The **Sad** side explains the difficult moment of saying good-bye to those that we were together with for years. We prayed and worshiped together, we shared each other happiness and sadness, we fought together for our rights! We believed that one day we would be together again.

From that night I remembered the dear faces that came to say "Good-bye". People were grouping in different corners of the house. Some were singing songs, others were sharing their last thoughts with us. The lights were on in the whole house for the most part of the night. It felt like nobody wanted to say the last word; neither step out of the house.

People started to leave all the way in the morning, right before dawn; they were walking out slowly, one by one, dropping their last tears. When the last "Good-bye" was said I fell on the bed as tired as dead. My feet were burning from standing for most of the night; my head was heavy as a rock. I was trying to fall asleep and give my tired body rest, but I couldn't. My heart was filled with such excitement that I couldn't close my eyes for a long time. It was a triumphant glorious moment of victory after long and exhausting fight! I don't remember how long I had been awake, but then the fatigue took over me and I slipped into a short but deep sleep.

Journey Through Life

It was five AM when the alarm put me back on my feet. We had to get up and do our final preparations. When the last item was packed in my suitcase, I glanced at the empty rooms that accommodated my family for years. The house looked empty and strangely comfortless with everything taken out of it. "Looks as empty, as some people's souls," I was thinking. "Sometimes we don't see from outside the emptiness that people have in their hearts." Then I walked out and took a look at the house of my childhood from the street. So much had happened in this house, so many memories stored. I was born under this roof; this was the only house that I knew in my entire life…Some kind of magnet wouldn't let me walk away from it. I was staring at the house and the backyard for quite a while. I was "hypnotized" by the memories that tied me to that place. This was the end of the first period of my life and now it was time to move on… to a better and brighter future. I put my head down and walked into the door for the last time.

Everybody was still running back and forth trying to pick up the last items from the floor in order to squeeze them into the overfilled suitcases. Suitcases didn't look nice and flat any more, all of them looked like balloons that could pop at any moment. The time of departure was approaching. Car drivers were anxiously waiting for us outside of the gate, "Hurry, hurry, please… it's time to leave!" We knelt down and asked God for protection in this important change in our life. Then we finished loading our luggage; it wasn't much, just two suitcases per person. Of course, for seven of us we got fourteen of them. The other two families took care of their luggage themselves. In about an hour we were on the highway, heading in the direction of Russian Customs. It took about six hours for us to get to the Customs.

XXIII. An Unexpected Chase

We were on the way to the border of the country and had no idea that the KGB plotted something terrible against our family. When our crew left the town, the KGB decided to follow us and either destroy our plans or cause any harm. This mad and godless gang was planning to fabricate an accident with us. Everything they wanted was to disturb or at least to delay our "exodus". They didn't care of the outcome of the operation, as long as that would create a reason to slow us down. One thing they didn't know, that their "crafty" skills would not interfere with God's perfect plan for His children. Just in a short distance before they caught up with us, the KGB car driver lost control of the steering wheel and crashed into a tree. This unsuccessful chase ended up with serious injuries of their crew. Meanwhile, we successfully proceeded in our way until we reached the custom port. How did we know about it? One of the members of their gang confessed later.

My dear reader, do you remember the story from the Bible when Moses was escorting Jewish slaves out of Egypt and Pharaoh's army was chasing the Jews in order to kill them? If you've never read this story, believe me, this is one of the greatest Bible stories that I have ever read. Pharaoh's heart was hardened and he didn't want to hear God's voice. God spoke to him many times through His messenger Moses asking him to free up the Jewish slaves. However, after all the troubles that came on Egypt, including the death of firstborns, Pharaoh had no choice, but to let Jews go. Soon after they left he regretted his decision and decided to make a chase after the Jews. When the Jews reached Red Sea, they discovered that they were not alone. The hunters under Pharaoh's leadership were approaching really fast. Being trapped between the Sea in front of them and Egyptian enemies behind them, the hearts of God's people squeezed

Journey Through Life

in fear. Moses lifted his arms up and asked God to deliver them out of this trap. God divided the Sea for Moses and the Jews and they were able to successfully cross it. As soon as Jews went into the Sea, Pharaoh's army followed them right behind. When the last Jewish slave stepped out of the Sea, God performed another miracle, saving His people from the furious army. The same way as God opened the Sea, the same way He closed the split of the Sea and heavy waves fell on the heads of Pharaoh's army. This was an act of God's salvation for the people who worshipped Him and the judgement to those who refused to listen to Him.

The Moses exodus story from the Bible has a lot of similarities with our exodus from the communist world. The same way as God protected Jews from the army of Pharaoh drowning them into the depth of the Sea, the same way God protected my family and friends from the furious KGB chasers, crashing them into a tree.

Many times when we pray and believe in God's protection and power, He surrounds us with an invisible army of angels and nothing can break through His circle of security. Oh, mighty and powerful God, I wish to worship you day and night and to glorify Your Holy Name! Praise be to Your Name among many nations forever and ever! Amen!

XXIV.   Crossing the "Red Sea"

Our final checkpoint in the Soviet Union was Chop. Chop was a customs city between the Soviet Union and Czechoslovakia; we called it "entrance to the foreign Europe". It's a very busy city that transports travelers to and from my country. If you could sit down on a bench and watch the city life, it would look like a commercial advertisement of luggage and other things related to the life of a traveler. At my spare time I liked watching busy areas of humanity, and the travel center was one of the busiest areas. All kind of panoramas would open up to my sight…How could that poor lady drag that huge suitcase that was almost her size? Oh… Look at that man! Not only is he holding the hands of his three children, but he also manages to pull with his own body a carriage full of suitcases. Just like a human horse! Some others wouldn't exhaust themselves physically. They would hire a porter at a small charge and enjoy their waiting time in the city. I wished that I could get a ride on a helicopter and look at the view from above. It would probably look like an anthill in its busy moment.

At the border a few concerns came up. Our biggest concern was how to get through the customs without further problems. I heard from other people experiences that Russian customs was a tough "search engine". They would search you through in and out. We all signed up at the customs' post and sat down waiting for our turn. We had to wait for hours… I didn't want anything to go wrong any more, so I was praying in my mind: "God, please be with us at this turning point of our lives. Please help us get through customs and bless our future. You performed many miracles for us already and you said that you will walk with us across the mountains and we will not fall. You will walk with us on the water and we will not drown, You will walk with us through the valley of the shadows and we will not be left alone. I know that You always keep Your words. You said, "Earth and sky will be destroyed, but the words I have said will never be destroyed." – Mark 13:31.

Deeply thinking of God's promises and the Scripture, I didn't notice how the time passed by. I turned my head when I heard the voice, coming out of the customs booth: "the Marchuk family is next." We all got up from the bench and formed a line in front of the customs office. The customs officer asked me to put the luggage on the running line and he searched it all looking in every tiny pocket and searching every fold that luggage could possibly have. After the luggage they searched our purses, pockets, they even asked us to remove shoes... Finally, we were free and clear to go to the other side of the customs – praise God; we were half free from the Communist system! Although, we were still within reach, we believed that God is our protection.

On Czechoslovakian side of the station we had to wait a few hours longer for the scheduled train. We couldn't wait to get on the train, so we could move further away from the country we used to call our homeland. What if the authorities decided to reverse their decision? What if they regret letting us go so easy? All kind of fearful thoughts still chased us as an anxiety to the Communist regime. God didn't let the chasers go further behind us.

Soon an operator announced that the passengers could board the train. Excited and inspired by the promising future, we slowly moved to the platform. All our hopes and dreams were brought to one point – leave the country of persecution and start a brand new life in a place where we could open our mouths and say word "God" without fear for life.

In the train we discovered that there weren't any available passenger seats. The only place that could accommodate us was the luggage compartment. How could this happen? I knew that we traveled at the full price of the ticket. Why were we squeezed into a luggage compartment? After all, we didn't care about the discomfort as long as the train was bringing us closer to our unseen future. Soon we got adjusted to our new "house on wheels", trying to make beds out of suitcases, looking for softer ones to place under our heads. It doesn't matter if we were considered "luggage", as long as we were moving toward our goal, we were fine. Exhausted from the events of that day and the previous night of a short sleep, I was asleep very fast.

The morning brightness woke me up and at first, I couldn't figure out where I was. Then my brain told me: "Celebrate, you are not in Russia any more!" My heart jumped, it was too good to be true! I didn't know how to express the feelings that I had at that moment, the feelings of freedom! Imagine a bird that was born in a cage and never had a chance to fly. The wings became useless, there was no need for them any more...And one day someone forgot to lock the door of the cage and the bird was free to fly anywhere under the sun! Like those caged birds, we were locked and burdened under heavy Communism. Free choice did not exist there and was not allowed! Everyone was supposed to follow the pre-designed mentality of the system! And one day, the powerful hand of God opened the door of the cage and we were free! I felt like I grew wings and as soon as I lift them, I would fly with the birds between the clouds, higher and higher into the sky. "Oh, my dear God, how beautiful is the world that you designed and it's even more beautiful in a harmony with freedom!" I looked at the sky again. The sun was slowly climbing up and brightening the world with its powerful rays. It was a gorgeous spring morning of May sixteen, nineteen eighty-eight. My body was sore and muscles ached from sleeping on a bumpy "bed", but my heart rejoiced. The train was running between fields of flowers and nice deep forests and I enjoyed every second of that morning. In an hour or so we arrived in the heart of Czechoslovakia, Prague. It was the beginning of a new chapter in my life.

According to the way sponsorship worked for Russian refugees, we were supposed to go through some waiting period in Europe before we get to the United States. Although, it was kind of unsettled life, but we enjoyed that time of travels very much. It was like a free vacation from Sweepstakes. We stayed in Vienna, Austria, for two weeks. Vienna is one ancient European City and the beautiful one. Its beautiful historical buildings designed in an antique architectural style, museums, streets made out of red stones will catch anybody's attention. It was also one of the cleanest cities that I ever visited. I don't remember seeing single pieces of trash anywhere on the ground. Everything was well maintained and taken care of. I was impressed of how this nation cared for their country.

Our next stop was Rome, Italy, and this was the final point of our European journey. We spent the rest of the summer in a beautiful Italian resort Ladispoli right on the Mediterranean Sea. Rome was only twenty miles away, therefore, we got a chance to travel back and forth. Rome – the powerful imperial city of those times when Jesus was walking on this planet! How many historical events took place in this city! Many of Rome's memorials and monuments reminded me of the time of Jesus. I wished that I could turn the time clock back into the past and become a disciple or at least a live witness of Jesus miraculous deeds on the earth. The disciples were the most blessed people who had an access to Jesus and who really had the closest personal relationship with Him. This was the time of grace. In the later years many of the followers of Jesus were tortured and murdered in the most terrible ways. Some of them were fed to wild animals on Rome's arenas; some were burned on the crosses. Nero, the bitter enemy of Christians, designed all kinds of entertaining scenes killing Jesus followers. Today

Jesus is not walking with us physically, but He is always with us in spirit. He guides and protects us in our ways every time we call upon Him. Let us praise Him forever!

Two months in Italy flew away really fast. As I said, it was the nicest period of my life: ocean, beach, beautiful summer days and also fellowship with Christian refugees from different places of my country. But the time had come for us to say: "Good-bye, Italy!"

It was August fifth, nineteen eighty-eight, when we landed in New York. The first sight that I saw in the New World was the Statue of Liberty. I felt like the statue was talking to me, saying the following words: "Give me your tired, your poor, your huddled masses yearning to breathe free, the wretched refuse of your teeming shore. Send these, the homeless, tempest-tost to me. I lift my lamp beside the golden door!" Large drops of tears rolled down my cheeks. It wasn't a dream anymore; it was a real free world that God initially designed for all born under the sun. "Is this really happening to us? Not just somebody else, but us?"

Dear reader, did you ever get a chance to win a lottery, or get inheritance from your rich uncle, or maybe you got a lucky number on the wheel of fortune? All of the above is nothing in comparison to how Jesus can bless you in your life if you give Him your heart!

Part II
New World

XXV. Adapting to the New World

While the church bus was running towards Philadelphia, I was impatiently looking in the window and counting down the miles. I wanted to be the first one to recognize the city. Philadelphia – the city of brotherly love, the city that I dreamed about for so long! Either because I couldn't find love in the surroundings that I grew up or because I was so excited about our exodus, the word Philadelphia was just like a sip of water in a hot desert. Maybe I expected to see painted hearts everywhere on the buildings? Or perhaps, I was looking for XOXO patterns? I wasn't quite sure what my heart was expecting but it was thirsty for a brotherly love. We took an exit to Philadelphia and soon the van was rolling on one of the largest streets – Roosevelt Boulevard. Through the evening shadows that were covering up the city I focused my eyes like the laser beams at every object that I could see outside. I remember seeing the whole line of trees that were separating the right lanes from the left ones. "Is that a city or a garden?" I thought. "Looks pretty and very spacious." We didn't get to cross the whole city on the first day because our sponsoring church was located in the northeast area of Philadelphia.

Our sponsors did a really great job helping us from A to Z and with everything we needed. Due to the size of our family, we were divided in two groups. Half of our family was temporarily placed in the church area with the beds located on the attic of the church's kitchen. It was awfully hot there during those August nights. I was the lucky one to find a better stay in someone's house. But still it gets hot everywhere when the heat goes over hundred Fahrenheit, unless you have good air conditioning system in your house. In the house where I stayed with my sister and parents air conditioning didn't work well at all. I remember waking up from a sweat bath and trying to find some kind of relief. I would go to the bathroom and wet my pajamas with cold water completely, but this system wouldn't last. In ten to twenty minutes my clothes would dry up on me from the body heat. It was kind of adjustment... I didn't expect that Pennsylvania could get that hot! I never experienced that kind of heat in my life, because I was born in a very cold country where the temperatures would never get higher than eighty – eighty two degrees. Never in my previous life I had to experience long-lasting hundreds of Fahrenheit in combination with extreme humidity. Since our arrival took place in early August (I was told that this was the hottest August ever), I had to build immunity against these unusually burning temperatures. All right, we were going through some tests in the New World. We were still living on the Earth. Only Heaven could offer a problem free environment, called paradise.

On the sixth day of my arrival to the United States I was brought to Karton Remanufacturing Industries and was offered a job. The job didn't look very attractive to my eyes, but I was thankful for everything that I could get at that time with my limited language skills. The job was in the Core Division of the company that was located in one of the unattractive neighborhoods of Philadelphia. When I looked at all those brown buildings with all kind of writings and paintings on the walls, I felt kind of uncomfortable. Trash was lying around the sidewalks and in the middle of the streets, old trolleys were pulling their wagons full of people. You could barely find someone to say "Hi" to you. All of this seemed to be discouraging. Is this what America all about? May be it was just my imagination? And yet, the people inside of the building where I worked were much friendlier. They ignored the fact that I didn't speak English much and were trying to help me as much as they could. I was grateful

Journey Through Life

for all the motivation and encouragement that I could receive from the complete strangers and thanked God in my heart. Although the job that I was doing was dirty and required a lot of physical strength, I promised myself that I was not going to quit, because this was the way to make it. Another thing that I had to get used to was the summer heat.

Every day I would go to work where I had to learn how to differ one core part from the other and sort them all in the proper baskets. I would receive trays and trays of dirty and rusty metal on the conveyor and had to make sense out of them. Climbing up and down on the metal baskets, trying to sort heavy calipers, I looked like a monkey that climbs from one tree to the other. I had to wear a helmet to prevent my head from an injury, an apron and big rubber gloves to protect me from dirt and scratches, but all of these safety gadgets would make me feel even hotter in the non-air-conditioned building. If you add to all the odds the smell of the oily grease (lubricants, used by the factory), you would imagine that this wasn't the lifestyle that I dreamed of. At the end of my working shift, when I had to remove the helmet, my hair would messily stick to my head and my clothes would be completely wet from the sweat caused by the extreme heat.

Right after work I had to catch two buses and a trolley in order to get to the evening school in time. All the energy that I had was used up for work, school and efforts of dealing with the unbeatable heat. At night I would have nightmares about intruders in my house. I would wake up in a fear and would wake my parents up too. My father would search the house and check the door locks, everything would be in place and the house would be peaceful and quiet as always. Some other nights I would wake up, finding myself with two perfume bottles in my hands. It was because in my dream I would compare two calipers and would try to find similarities or differences between them. Day after day, night after night in the same tough circle...

I knew that all the nightmares were caused by the stress but the desire to survive in the New World took a lead. I dreamed of changing this difficult circle of my everyday existence, but didn't know how. I didn't have the answer yet. I learned to be patient, to wait and see what time would bring. For the time being I to had to study and work at the utmost of my strength to get to the better future. No matter how hard it was at the beginning, I had my dream focused in the right direction.

One of the highest priorities for me was to learn English as fast as I could. I took evening college classes in the Community College of Philadelphia. In three months I got some basic skills and was able to communicate and even translate to others. Since there were a lot of Russian people coming to the United States at that time, I kind of played a role of a volunteer interpreter to them. You could see me accompanying somebody in different areas, such as real estate, INS, work places, schools and the list goes on and on... Often I would go to the airport to meet newcomers. After all, I was very familiar with the Philadelphia airport and also the Kennedy airport in New York. My schedule was tightly incorporated into schedules of many others in Russian community. If anybody had a housing issue they would call me. I would represent people in any of the government offices (Social Security Administration, Immigration and Naturalization Services), people would turn to me again and again with all kind of requests. In my working place I was that kind of link, that handled all the disputes between the employer and Russian people. Even in the later days, when people got settled and learned some communication skill, they would still come to me with their problems. They gave me a title of their unofficial attorney, because I always tried to help.

Journey Through Life

When I think back sometimes, I tried to figure out how I did that? From the time of our arrival to the US there were so many people arriving from my homeland. Everybody was looking for freedom and especially religious freedom. After two or three months there was quite a team of Russians and Ukrainians at the place where I worked. There were many others that were trying to come to America, but were still on the waiting list. All of my friends were very concerned about their family members, that also wanted to come here, but couldn't find the sponsors. With all of those concerns for my people I came up with an idea to write a letter to the owner of the company, Mr. Karton. With the help of the dictionary I put together a letter expressing the needs and the problems of the people. I asked if Mr. Karton could assist this worried crowd in any way he could during this difficult time of transition. My letter touched the owner's heart. Being away from the city, he sent the Director of Human Resources to meet with me on his behalf. Frank, one of the nicest people that I knew, listened to me patiently. He asked me to feel free to contact him at any time and he would address as many problems as he could. Shortly after the meeting with Frank, I met with Mr. Karton. This humble and people-loving Christian employer did a lot of good things for my people and me. He even went to Italy to meet with other Russian immigrants and offered them his sponsorship and jobs.

XXVI. The Speech at Pennsylvania University

Our family was one of the first families that arrived to Philadelphia from the Soviet Union. Due to the political changes in the Soviet Union at that time with Gorbachev coming to power, many Americans learned such words as "perestroika" (reconstruction) and "glasnost" (publicity). This subject was really "hot" in US media. We found out that some reporters were interested in meeting with my family and one day I was introduced to Action News (ABC channel 6) in Philadelphia. I had an excellent interpreter that helped me say everything in a few words. Later that evening I was really amazed to see my face on TV.

A few weeks later I was invited to share my testimony in another faculty – the University of Pennsylvania. I spoke in front of an audience of students and professors. An African-American student served as my interpreter, I couldn't believe that he could speak Russian so well! I remember everybody's eyes were anxiously looking at me when I started to speak and I felt such an inspiration that I kept going and going. I had a lot to say about my unusual life experiences. I finished my testimony with the story "The Carpenter". This was one of my favorite stories. "An elderly carpenter was ready to retire. He told his employer-contractor of his plans to leave the house-building business and live a more leisurely life with his wife enjoying his extended family. He would miss the paycheck but needed to retire. They could get by.

The contractor was sorry to see his good worker go and asked if he could build just one more house as a personal favor. The carpenter said, "Yes". But in time it was easy to see that his heart was not in his work. He resorted to shoddy workmanship and used interior materials. It was an unfortunate way to end a dedicated career.

Journey Through Life

When the carpenter finished his work, the employer came to inspect the house and handed the front door key to the carpenter. "This is your house," he said. "My gift to you."

The carpenter was shocked! What a shame! If he had only known that he was building his own house, he would have done it all so differently!

And so it is with us... We build our lives, a day at a time, often putting less than our best into the building. Then with a shock we realize we have to live in the house we have built. If we could do it over, we'd do it much differently. But we cannot go back...

You are the carpenter. Each day you hammer a nail, place a board, or erect a wall. "Life is a do-it-yourself project," someone has said. Your attitude and your choices you make today, build the "house" you live in tomorrow...So build wisely!"

Then I stopped... It was such a silence that you could hear a squeaky cricket sound coming somewhere from outside. After a few seconds my audience realized that this was the end of my story and the loud applause tore the silence. Students came to greet and welcome me; they thanked me for sharing my story with them. I even got a gift from Professor Eric – it was a series of books "Chronicles of Narnia". This was a very encouraging experience for me and I will never forget it. Telling you the truth, I am always ready to share my testimony about miracles that Jesus performed in my life. I don't think I will ever get tired of doing that. That is why I decided to write this book. Unlike the carpenter, I have to build my house the best I can, so I could enter the eternal paradise with Jesus. God bless you, my dear reader. May He touch your heart for you to understand the depth of His love.

XXVII.   My Important Friends

I have to tell you, dear reader, about one extraordinary family from Moscow, that played a huge role in our successful immigration. I was really blessed to meet two of the greatest people who sacrificed almost everything for one good purpose – to help Christians get their freedom. Their efforts and love for people could be compared to the works of Martin Luther King, Jr., however, were never recognized by Russian authorities.

Vasily, one of the top federal officers in Moscow used to belong to the highest league of Russian government. Being a regular companion of the former Russian President Leonid Brezhnev, Vasily was very proud of the level he reached in his life. His wife Galina, a bright and lovely woman, worked as a professor of the highest University of Moscow. Everything was going fine for this family until Vasily was assigned one of the government secret cases. When he studied the case, he found that it was pulled into a dirty government affair. Finding himself in the middle of the dirty political battle, Vasily didn't know what to do. As a truthful and honest person, he felt that he was trapped in a political web. One side of him was telling him to block his ears from the voice of conscience just like everybody else did and to go with the flow. But the other side of him was not agreeing with this decision. He pulled all his strength together trying not to think about it, however, every night he was waking up from nightmares. May be his conscience talked to him at night. His wife saw that something was bothering her husband and asked him if everything was all right. Due to the extreme secrecy of the case, he couldn't even share anything with his lovely wife. He had to battle it alone. He thought that time would erase images of the dirty government affairs from his mind, but so far nothing worked for him. All his trust and beliefs in Russian government were crushed. He felt robbed, cheated and empty. Russian government, the highest leading level of the nation, should be the most ideal and truthful example of all, however, it was not. "Where is that place where truth resides? Where do I go to find it?" With these thoughts in his head Vasily decided to go through yellow pages for communities and organizations that could give him "the formula of truth". He wished that there was a section in the telephone book that would say, "Most truthful and honest organizations of the country," but there wasn't one. He had to do it the hard way, hoping that someone would give him advice. Wandering around the neighborhoods he couldn't figure out where to go and who to ask.

One day when Vasily was driving on one of the quiet streets of Moscow, he heard a sound of a wonderful choir accompanied by an organ. The sweet sounds of the song made him stop and listen for few minutes. That sound reminded him of one of the songs that his mother sang for him when he was a child. Listening to that wonderful choir he started daydreaming. His memories brought him into his childhood field. He remembered running between the trees and trying to hide from his mother in the tall grass. His mother would find him, grab his hand and they would run between the trees together. They would stop frequently, running out of breath. Then they would sit down in the grass and pick up some beautiful flowers that would spread aroma for miles. Sitting on the mother's lap, he would feel loved and secured. His mother would sing him a song and he wouldn't think of a bigger joy that he had at that moment. Beautiful innocent childhood will never lose its brightness in his memory album.

A sudden signal of a car awakened him from daydreaming and brought him back to reality. He realized that he parked in the middle of the street blocking the way. Vasily slowly pulled into the parking lot. Hypnotized by his childhood memories he came out of the car and went inside of the building.

It was a large building made out of stone from the early twentieth century and looked like an old church. Looking around and studying the place, he walked into a big room, which was supposed to be the fellowship hall. Inside, he found a group of people singing and worshiping God. A few ushers met him at the door and invited him to sit down. "Who are these people and what are they doing here? Who is that God whose name they mention all the time?" After a few songs and the introduction part, a minister came up on the platform and started to read from a book. He read, "Jesus said, "I am the Way and the Truth and the Life. And who follows me will find the truth and the way and will inherit an eternal life."

The minister was going on and on, talking about a mysterious Jesus, who can answer all the questions and who can give an abundant life. "Who is this Jesus, that promises all these wonderful things to people? Where do I find him?" Vasily was thinking.

Meanwhile, the minister was talking about all the wonderful things that Jesus promised to people. "What Jesus could give to those who accept Him is much more valuable than what the world could offer or even than life itself! Whoever met with Jesus cares less about what happens to him on the earth. I would like to share with you a Melinda's story. A young couple was deliriously happy when a beautiful little girl was born. This young couple was unsaved; in fact, they had somehow grown to hate anything and everything that had anything to do with God, and His Son Jesus Christ. Instead of doing as they should, and presenting the baby to the Lord for His blessing, they made a vow that the little girl, whom we shall call Melinda, was never to be allowed exposure to anything that had anything to do with Christianity.

Journey Through Life

Throughout her young girlhood she wasn't allowed to go to Sunday School. If a preacher or soul winner from a local church visited their home, Melinda was sent to her room, before the visitors were let in. Melinda's parents and grandparents were well to do; and she had more toys and dolls than she could keep up with and ate only the best of foods and wore the very best clothing money could buy. Her parents made sure of her secular and cultural training. She studied piano, voice and ballet with the best teachers and instructors money could afford; but her parents were doing a very good job of keeping her away from learning anything about the Lord.

One-day Melinda's mother was baking her husband a birthday cake, and she discovered that she lacked a certain ingredient. She called her beautiful nine-year old daughter, gave her some money and sent her to the store to purchase the ingredient. Her orders were that the girl should go straight down the street to the store, purchase the article and come straight home. Melinda, glad to be going out on the sunny spring day, skipped down to the street, went into the store, purchased the article, and started back home. Melinda decided that it might be fun to take a different route home, so she turned left at an intersection and walked up a back street. She knew that it would intersect a little farther up with the street that would lead to her home, so no harm could come out of it. As she walked along, she began to hear some pretty singing and music, and the farther she walked, the louder it became. Finally, she saw that the singing and music was coming from a big building just across the street from her. Melinda loved music and singing, and she possessed the natural curiosity of a nine-year old, so she crossed the street and entered the building."

While listening to the story, Vasily was shocked that the story was really similar to his! Just like that little girl, he happened to pass by the building that attracted him with the singing that came out of it. It sounded really interesting, therefore, he sharpened his ears and continued to listen with more attention and interest that was growing inside of him. The ministered continued telling the story, "Though Melinda didn't know it, this was a mission house, and inside was a goodly number of down-and-outers: a cross section of the folks from the lower echelon of society; but many seated there had experienced the regenerating power of receiving Jesus Christ into their lives. Some were there just fulfilling their obligation for having been given breakfast, and perhaps some article of clothing. As Melinda shyly entered, they looked back and smiled at the beautiful little girl.

She sat down in back, thinking she would stay just a little while and listen to the group on the podium singing such a beautiful song, but one she had never heard before. The group finished their song, and a pleasant-faced gentleman came to the podium and welcomed the assemblage. After a word of prayer, he began to preach.

Melinda knew that she should get up, and hurry on home, but something seemed to hold her to her seat. The preacher was talking about who Jesus is, and the many compassionate miracles He performed, and finally describing his arrest and cruel treatment by the Roman soldiers and King Herod Antipa's guards, and finally His crucifixion. "At that very time of year when lambs were being sacrificed for a covering for sin, Jesus Christ became the Lamb of God; not to cover our sins, but take them away. Jesus had never committed a sin as we have, but He took all our sins to the cross, and was nailed there: shedding His precious blood to cleanse us from all sin and make us ready to go to Heaven." The missionary preached on about why it was necessary for Christ to come down to earth and give us His life on Calvary's cross to pay our sin debt.

Tears flowed from Melinda's beautiful hazel eyes. The singing group came back to the podium to join the

Journey Through Life

missionary, the piano started up, and they began to sing "There's Room at the Cross for You." After the first verse of chorus the missionary began the altar call with the group singing softly behind him, "Some of you have gone too long, living your life without Jesus and His wonderful gift of salvation," he said. "Here at the mission house we have offered many of you gifts of food, shelter and articles of clothing. You accepted these gifts, and we're glad; but a greater gift is being offered: the greatest gift ever offered to anyone. The free gift of salvation. And with that gift another wonderful thing comes to pass: you are adopted into the family of God and become joint heirs with Christ."

Melinda found herself walking down the aisle to the altar in front of the podium. Her face was streaked with tears. A lady knelt beside Melinda and hugged her, then took her Bible and quietly explained how she could give her heart and life to Jesus and be saved. Melinda repeated the sinner's prayer. There was "joy unspeakable and full of glory" in Melinda's heart as she left the mission house.

When she had started from her home there was a warm sun shining, but now a cold rain was pouring down. Melinda knew she would be punished for being gone so long and worrying her parents. By the time she arrived home her pretty dress was drenched, and her blonde curls hung limp down the side of her face. She shivered. Melinda's mother angrily jerked her around to face her, plying her with questions about where she had been so long. Her father came in with an expression on his face that scared Melinda. Finally, she spoke, "Mama-Daddy, I am sorry I worried you by being gone so long, but I have something wonderful to tell you. I heard some pretty singing and music, and went inside a building. They told me all about Jesus dying on a cross. Mama-Daddy, I gave my heart to Jesus and..." Melinda was interrupted by a loud anguished sound coming from deep in her father's throat. He uttered blasphemous profane exclamations, and became, as a man possessed. Melinda had never seen her father like that: then she saw him strip off his heavy belt and approach her. Melinda's mother wept in loud cries as her husband beat her daughter until she fell to the mercifully passing out. For two days Melinda was confined to her bedroom. The harsh beating had left not only bruises, but also some lacerations. Her mother applied ointments and alcohol rub, saying very little, sometimes with tears in her eyes.

The morning of the third day, Melinda awakened with a raging fever and raspy breathing. A doctor was summoned; his diagnosis being double pneumonia. These were the days before penicillin was available. Several medications were tried, but Melinda's condition only worsened. The fever raged on; and Melinda moved in and out of consciousness; sometimes murmuring bits and pieces of the wonderful things she had heard at the mission. Her mother sat by her bed patting her forehead with a cold cloth. The doctor came by briefly, leaving the room sadly shaking his head. Just before dark Melinda sat up in bed and called for her mother. Her mother had lost a lot of sleep and had dozed off when she was awakened by Melinda's call. When she saw her sitting up in bed it gave her a happy start. She thought the fever had broke and there would be a chance for Melinda to recover after all.

"Mama," Melinda said softly. "Yes, sweetheart; I'm here." "Mama, I want you to bring me the dress I was wearing that day." "No, honey," her mother groaned. "You don't want to see that thing. It was soiled and torn-and-had some bloodstains on it. I threw it in the trash." "Please Mama; go and get it for me." "But why, Melinda?" Her mother protested. Melinda's father appeared in the doorway of the bedroom with guilt and grief written all over his haggard face. Melinda has lain back down again, closing her eyes. She hadn't seen her father enter. She spoke softly,

Journey Through Life

but loud enough for both parents to hear her final words on earth. "Mama, an angel came and told me I would be going to Heaven soon. I wanted to take the dress with me so I could show Jesus that I shed some blood for Him just like He shed for me..."

The Melinda story told by the minister touched Vasily's heart. Tears were bursting out of his eyes, but he didn't want to show his sensitivity to the congregation and bowed his head down for nobody to see his wet face. After the service Vasily decided to introduce himself to the minister, who actually was the pastor of that church. Vasily asked him all the questions that were nested in his head for quite awhile. The Pastor invited him to sit down and then he slowly explained the basics of the Bible. He explained that the Bible carries answers for all the situations of people's lives. After the meeting pastor gave him the Bible.

Impressed by all the events happening to him in the past few hours, Vasily walked out of the building, carrying the Bible in his hands and new hope in his heart.

He shared his experience with his wife Galina. After hearing her husband's story she was anxious to find out about that church for herself. Vasily spent the whole week reading the New Testament of the Bible and the more he read the more he desired to read it. The incident with the church and the reading of the Bible opened a new page in Vasily's life. He went back to the church the following Sunday because he knew what he wanted to do. He made the decision to accept Christ and to join the church. His wife Galina united her heart with her husband's decision and accepted Christ too. Their life changed drastically: when they both found Christ, they found new life and the way to the truth. Their understanding of life changed. All their interests and desires became focused on living for Christ. The fact of giving their lives to Christ brought a whole chain of issues in their material world.

As soon as the government found out about the changes in Vasily's life, they immediately dismissed him from his high government position. Communist government would not accept anything religious, because they considered religion and Christianity a disease that could be contagious to others. "Christianity is an infection that could spread around and cause a decay in people's heads. Anything that is religious, especially on the high level, must be aborted!"

It was a high fall for Vasily from the highest rank of government straight to the ground. In spite of this, he didn't get hurt. Jesus was right there catching him and holding him in His powerful arms. Galina experienced the similar thing. She lost her teaching career at the University. They would even try to take away her professor's abilities if they could.

Vasily and Galina had to make major adjustments to their lifestyle before their bank savings ran out. They had to move from their villa to a small affordable apartment. That was the time when I met with this couple.

When Ronald Reagan came to Moscow to meet with Russian president Chernenko, Vasily and Galina were scheduled to meet with American government too. The most outrageous government officers did everything that was in their power to prevent Americans from meeting with this brave family. Vasily and Galina were captured by the authorities and sent blindfolded thousands of miles away from Moscow right before Reagan's visit. They were placed under a home arrest in a small Ukrainian town, away from highways and major cities. They were released from their temporary "refuge place" as soon as Americans left The Soviet Union.

Time passed by and Michael Gorbachev became the new President in USSR. This election brought a huge change for people like this courageous family and many others. We finally received what we fought for – freedom to leave the country that would never accept our beliefs. We were free

Journey Through Life

to go anywhere in the world, where our rights and beliefs would be respected. Vasily and Galina got permission to immigrate to Canada and that's where I visited them soon after they arrived. I haven't heard from this great family since, but I am sure that God takes good care of them.

XXVIII. My Working Career Continues

After nine months of working in the Core department of Karton Remanufacturing, I was promoted to the Distribution department of the company, where I became a Supervisor for Calipers and Water Pump product lines. I really liked working with people and always helped everybody. Our department was like a family to me: we celebrated each other's birthdays, we greeted newcomers and arranged bridal or baby showers for the future brides and moms. I remember getting in a bus with a large playpen, that I just purchased from "Toys R Us". It was a gift for one of the mothers to be. We sure had a lot of fun together.

I even got in trouble few times defending people. There was one young Russian lady, Oksana, working on the Caliper packing line and she was about seven months pregnant. However, some of the supervisors would forget the fact that the expecting mom needed special attention and lighter work. The required quota had to be done every day. Oksana was on the same line of job with everybody else. She tried her best but due to her conditions, could not keep up with everybody. She fell behind her co-workers in her daily amount of work. One day she sat down on the line and started to cry. As a department leader, I needed to take care of the situation fast. I ran to her and tried to calm her down. Then I saw that all my efforts were worthless, I just added more wood to the fire. Her tears were not dropping any more, but rolling down her cheeks like two overflowing rivers. Since almost everyone in my department got involved in that issue, I decided to call all my team members for a meeting. I promised them that I would do everything that was in my strength for the supervisor to make a necessary change. Everyone who had any medical conditions may not

Journey Through Life

be required to make the same quota. They have to be placed on a light job and should not be under the same pressure as everyone else. When I finished the meeting, I found out that someone reported me to the Manager, David H. He was known as a nice and friendly person. I don't know what happened, but this time he lost his "cool"! He called me from his office and commanded that I should leave the department immediately. He said that he didn't wish to see me at my job any longer. Why? Why did he tell me that? Does he even know what I was trying to accomplish? I was really dejected, but found strength not to leave until the end of the day. When the bell rang at four PM, I picked up my belongings and went home in a state of confusion. I had no idea what I was going to do. Troubled by the events of that day, I felt very disappointed. That evening I was choking on my food at the dinner table, it wouldn't go down my throat.

After the dinner the phone rang and my mother answered the phone. "Galina," she said. Guess, who is calling? It's David H." "David?" I paused... "I am not sure if I want to talk to him." But then I took the phone from my mother's hands.

"Galina, I am so sorry for what told you today," his voice had a note of regret in it. "I realized my mistake and am seeking for your forgiveness. Could you forgive me?" He apologized over and over, he almost cried. He begged me to come back to work the next day as usual, and promised that he will never make the same mistake. I was shocked to hear this entire apology from my top boss, but was very relieved after that phone conversation. I felt that the stone rolled away from my heart and all the pressure came off me. That night I slept good, I needed to recover from that stressful day.

The next morning David was waiting for me. He gave me a friendly handshake and again asked to forgive him. He told me that the day before after I left work, a group of people from my department met with him and asked him to reverse his decision. He realized it himself too. I was pleased to hear that my people stood up for me.

Two representatives of the Human Resources department approached me that morning asking if there were any problems at my work the day before. I said that al the issues were resolved. I knew that the Bible teaches us to forgive and forget our offences. I couldn't cause any problems for him. As a result of that incident, Oksana was transferred to the department of light labor. Later, the procedures were revised and became effective for everyone who had special medical conditions.

XXIX. In a Search for the Other Half

The Bible says in Matthew 19:4-6 "When God made the world, He made them male and female. And God said, "So a man will leave his father and mother and be united with his wife, and the two will become one body. So there are not two, but one." Sometimes I was wondering where was the other half that God created for me? I had been around different countries, but never met my half yet! I was patient and knew that time will reveal it for me.

At that time I worked as a department leader in a packing department of the company. I loved caring for people and always did my best. There were people from different nationalities working for me and this was a wonderful experience. It's like a bouquet of flowers of all kind. I was learning about different cultures, different customs. I heard all kind of English accents and learned to understand everybody. There was a handful of Russian and Slavic speaking people and communication with them was as easy to me as one, two, and three. There were Spanish, Indians, Vietnamese, Americans, Cubans, Romanians, Portuguese and Haitian workers.

Alix, a quiet and respectful young man, always did an outstanding job in his work. As his supervisor, I noticed that he was one of the few top quota busters in the department. I was wondering how he did it without any unnecessary gestures or movements. He worked so calmly and quietly, but always accomplished more than his fussy co-workers. His hands were moving so fast that you wouldn't even catch it with your simple look. He was fast and efficient worker. For some reason, this quiet man got my attention. He didn't speak much, just answered shortly when he had to. I noticed that he seemed to be in another world. When I found out later, he had a lot in his mind at that time.

One day after spending vacation in Florida, I was showing everybody in the department photos that I took. When I showed them to Alix, he asked me who was the lady that I took pictures with. I told him that this was one of my best Russian friends. "Besides, I met some French speaking people in Fort Lauderdale," I said and I couldn't hold myself from making a joke. "I wouldn't have problems understanding them if you were there to interpret for me." He told me that the next time I go to Florida, he will be there and he will be on my photos with me instead of my Russian friend. I laughed at the joke, but was wondering if there was anything hiding behind that joke?

One day Alix handed me his phone number. I looked at him surprisingly, but said, "Thank you." I called him that evening and asked what that was all about. He said that he would like to meet with me and discuss a few things. I was kind of shocked, but there was something about Alix that I couldn't resist. He was such a "gentleman", that you will not find many around. Did he hypnotize me with his sophisticated respectful personality? I couldn't understand my feelings, but decided to meet with him. To my surprise, there was no meeting. I was waiting for half an hour, but he didn't show up. This made me even more curious.

"What happened?" I asked him on the next day at work. "Did you change your mind?"

"No", he said. "I thought that you changed your mind."

"I was waiting for you for an hour but you didn't show up!" I said.

Then I figured out that we were waiting for each other in two different places at the same time. Since it didn't work out, I said, "Well, this is not it. This was probably just the false alarm." Then Alix approached me at work and asked me again if we could meet. He felt kind of down. "All right,"

Journey Through Life

I said. "But please don't misplace the address this time." He smiled, "Don't worry. I will be there."

We met in a park and I got to know Alix better. The more I learned about him, the closer I was getting to him. We became really good friends. I talked to him about God and my wonderful experiences back in Russia. He mostly listened. He was a very polite person, funny speaker, and also a great listener. I enjoyed Alix's company, so he did mine. I felt very comfortable and pleasant when he was near, I didn't even notice when I fell for him.

My first impressions of Alix being quiet changed when he started to tell me stories from his life. Those stories draw my attention. I was kind of captured by his testimony and our roles switched, he became a speaker and I was a listener. In my mind I was drawing pictures of places where he had been and imagining the faces of people that he told me about. It was like watching an imaginary movie accompanied by the soft voice of a narrator.

"Since nineteen eighty eight God wanted to take my attention," he said.

"So what happened?" I asked. "Did you reject Him at that time?"

"Kind of... But I just want you to hear the full story and you will see."

He calmly continued his story and I was listening and absorbing it's every detail. "As a young man, I was a little stubborn sometimes. Even though I knew the Lord, but I never paid attention to the people who were divine inspired and could foretell the future of someone. You wouldn't believe what happened to me, proud young man that only believed in himself and only trusted his own judgments," he looked at me with the corner of his eyes.

"All right, please continue, I am ready to hear all of it!" I expressed slight impatience, because I was completely plugged into his story.

He looked at me with a smile and continued, "One day at the beginning of nineteen eighty-eight my life started to shift in a new direction when my aunt Rosette came to me and told me that I had to reverse the decision that I made recently. Guess what my decision was?" he hesitated for a few seconds. "I wanted to marry a girl that I met two years before. God revealed to my aunt in her dream that it was not a good decision because God planned something else for me. She shocked me with her revelation but I was in love with the girl. How could she dare to say something like that? After all I was grown up and didn't have to mind anyone that couldn't please me. I was almost convinced. At the same time, I was disturbed to some degree and a little confused. But my stubborn mind told me to follow my initial decision and I did.

"What do you know about my future, and who is that God that tells you that? Keep your prophecies to yourself, but I am not changing my mind. I love this girl as much as she loves me and very soon we will be happily married couple."

She replied, "My son, you know that I love you and I am not trying to hurt you, because everything I told you is the truth. God told me also that if you didn't listen, your marriage would only last for six months. When this happens, this would be a sign for you that this revelation is true and real."

At this point I didn't want to argue with her any more. I said, "Fine" and left. That evening when I got to my bed, I couldn't sleep. For some reason my aunt's warning bothered me, but I was trying to calm myself down. "Why wouldn't God approve this marriage," I thought. "I love her and she loves me and what could be the problem with that? Besides, I was living a sinful life and wanted to stop that for my conscience not to judge me anymore. I am being very honest and sincere and want to stop any "wrongs" that I allowed to

Journey Through Life

happen in my life. Parties and sex started to get a bitter taste and I needed to change it badly. Why would God want to stop this marriage, this was the only solution to my problems?"

With full head of thoughts and arguments I fell asleep, hoping that the morning will shed new light on my problems. But the next day didn't bring anything new for me, neither the day after. My mother, who was a born again Christian, did not feel right about my marriage either, she even protested against it. In spite of everything, I proceeded with my plan and in November of nineteen eighty-eight I got married.

Everything seemed to be going well: the ceremony, the reception, and the honeymoon. We had a fantastic start and for the first few weeks we were living in our "American dream." I started to laugh at my doubts and was a little angry with my aunt. "Look at my life! I have everything I want and all my friends are jealous of me! If I listened to this lady, I would miss my chance!" Anyway, I was more than sure that I made the right choice. Regina (my wife) was sweet and caring, and she always cooked the best meals for me. The only thing that bothered me was that she loved to talk on the phone a lot.

On the second month of our marriage I noticed that she spent more time on the phone than she spent with me. Sometimes she would talk for hours and when I asked whom she was talking to, she would say that it was her childhood friend. Soon she started to travel often. I found out that she traveled from Pennsylvania to New York, which was two hours away from the place where we lived. At this point I began to wonder what was going on or why was she going to New York so often? When I asked her why did she go to New York all the time, she told me that she was visiting her girlfriend Albert, who was sick for a while. This answer didn't quite satisfy me and I decided to make a little investigation on my own. I wanted to look at my telephone bill, but I never got to it, because she was handling all the bills. I called the Phone Company and asked them to send a copy of my last bill to a different address.

Meanwhile, some other strange things started to happen between us. She moved out of the bedroom, excusing herself that my snoring kept her awake. I tried to talk her into moving back in, but she totally refused. At that point I remembered my aunt's dream and started to think that she could be right, because I saw that our marriage wasn't working out the way I expected. Regina continued sleeping in the other room, we communicated with each other briefly. I offered her to meet with a marriage counselor, but she disagreed. She seemed to make up her mind in whatever she was doing, but, surely, kept me out of that.

The following month I decided to go to New York for a weekend, but I patiently waited for her to leave first. I knew that she was going to New York again. When I got to New York, I let the time to go by until the evening and then called my wife's friend Albert (as I said before, Albert was Regina's girlfriend, although it sounds unusual for a girl's name). Regina was supposed to be visiting Albert due to Albert's poor health condition. Albert was happy to hear from me and asked me how was I doing and how was Regina? "Everything is all right," I replied. "By the way did Regina stop by your house? She told me this morning that she was going to see you." "Oh, no," she said. "She never got here yet. What time did she leave?" I looked at the time; it was ten thirty PM. Where in the world was she hanging around since this morning? Since I didn't want her friend to be suspicious of anything, I just said, "Well, she could be caught in a traffic. I will call back tomorrow." After this phone conversation I knew that Regina was not telling me the truth, why would she do that to me? What have I done wrong that pushed her in any wrong direction? I started to examine our married life from the first day, but besides the romance, roses and kindness to each other, I couldn't

Journey Through Life

find any cause for us to grow apart from each other. I was completely confused and frustrated and began to feel sick in my stomach. I was scared and weak and the words of my aunt started to hunt me, they were slowly eating me inside. I never thought that something would happen and especially that soon...

I woke up in the hotel room with the same feeling that I had the previous day. I still felt weak and could not eat anything. All I could do was to search for the missing puzzle of my marriage. I knew that somehow I would find some details. And I did."

Alix paused... I was gazing at his face. He was breathing heavily. I saw how much he was hurting and how deep was the wound of the betrayal from the person that he dearly loved. I didn't move... I just wanted him to pour out all of the pain that was in his heart, I was ready to take it. He sat silently for some time; I was very patient, giving him time to sort out the things in his mind. Then he realized that I was waiting for him to continue and something similar to a smile appeared on his face. He seemed to clear his throat and continued,

"After my meaningless trip to New York I went to see my mother. That's where I used to pick up some of my mail. This time I was really anxious to see what was in the mail for me. First thing that I saw was the telephone bill that I expected so badly. My heartbeats increased when I picked up that bill. I knew that I would get some truth from it. Well, here it was! The bill that totaled to a couple hundreds of dollars! All these money! Wait a minute! Fifty calls to one unknown number in New York? I couldn't match up that number to any of the numbers that I possibly ever wrote in our phone directory. Besides, this was not the number of her friend Albert, that she claimed calling all the time! I was furious!

The same evening I called the number from the telephone bill and a child answered the phone. I asked for Regina and the child answered, "She was here few minutes ago, but now she went to a party with Erold." Erold! Who was that mysterious Erold? I was stunned! Later I found out that Erold was her ex-boyfriend. I went out to our friends and her family members and asked if they knew anything about her seeing her ex-boyfriend? Some of them said, "Yes, we knew about it, but we couldn't change her mind." I knew it! I shouldn't be that naïve!

After few days spent in New York, she came back home with a wide smile on her face, so I could not confront her at that moment. But later I asked where did she stay in New York. She replied that she stayed with her friend.

"Lier," I said. "You didn't stay there, because I talked to her and she didn't even know that you were in the city. Therefore, where were you?"

"I stayed over Erold's family," she said.

"Why?"

"I don't know why," she said.

"I want you to quit this relationship with your ex, because I will not tolerate it while we are married." She did not respond.

However, she continued seeing her ex-boyfriend, there is nothing that I could do to change her mind. Finally, I approached her and asked her one last question,

"Are you sure that you are in love with this man?" She answered slowly and timidly with a smile on her face,

"Yes, I do."

You cannot imagine how I felt that day when my wife after four months of marriage was standing in front of me and telling me that she was in love with someone else. At that very moment all kinds of things went through my mind, but I reminded myself that God had warned me about it

Journey Through Life

before I got married. I had no choice but to withdraw myself from this relationship.

"I cannot stay with you in this apartment while you are having this relationship," I said. I packed up some clothes and moved out. She never showed me any reaction regarding my decision. Instead she told me that one-day I would thank her for what she did. I couldn't understand why she said that. To me she looked like someone confused. "She doesn't know what she is doing, nor even know what she is saying," I thought. I took my suitcase and moved to my mother's house for a temporary stay.

Two days after I moved out of the apartment I received a call from her friend. Her friend suggested that I drove to my wife's apartment right away, because the other man just moved in the apartment with her. I was shocked once again! In a rush I put my clothes on and drove to the building where just few months ago I shared my happiness with the person that vowed to be with me for the rest of our lives. I knocked in the door many times, but there was no response. I still had the key from the entrance door, so I pulled out the key from my pocket and pushed it into the lock. To my surprise, the lock was already changed! The lady that gave me her oath of love was really "thoughtful"! She sure did all the necessary steps to "protect her recurrent love" before her light mind gets tired of it. I could never figure out if she ever understood what the real love was. Perhaps, she was in a hurry to experience new adventures and never gave chance for the real love to come in.

I was still knocking in that door, saying,

"Open the door, I know that you are there."

Finally, I heard her voice from behind the door,

"Leave me alone! If you are not going to leave, I will call the police and report you as a rapist!"

I couldn't believe my own ears...What happened to this woman? She must have lost her mind! I didn't want to have any troubles with the police department, I already got enough from that wife of mine! I just left...

From that time I didn't know what to do anymore. I settled in my mother's house... I was losing weight due to the lack of appetite... I was in a stage of depression...I lost any interest for parties, I was indifferent to anything that was happening around me at that time period. I was locked in a triangle between my work, home and church that I visited more often with my mother. When I look back, I remember that I looked like a lost ship in the Bermuda triangle. At that time I didn't know if I could ever find strength to fight with the waves of raging waters; or the powerful waters would swallow my ship and would drop me deeply into the heart of the bottomless sea..."

This story of love, marriage and deception broke my heart. I took a deep sigh, but couldn't find any words to comfort him. I just sat there in a complete silence, he became silent too. It was getting late and the evening shadows were moving in slowly. Few stars appeared on the darkened sky. Our minds were floating somewhere in two different worlds. But for some reason I felt that in the midst of all that silence our worlds could communicate. I took his hand and tightly squeezed it; he gave me a look of appreciation. I used that moment to bring him back to the ground from his imaginary world.

I opened my mouth and almost whispered,

"Is that what had been bothering you all these days? Thank you for sharing it with me, I will keep you in my prayers." "You are welcome," he replied, "but if you let me, I'd like to tell you more..." "Of course!" I said. "I will be more than happy to hear the rest of your story." "Thank you," he said. "I needed to share it with someone..."

Then he continued,

"Days were passing by, day by day...I was waiting to see what direction my life would take from that crucial

Journey Through Life

intersection. To my disappointment, there was no change for a while; every day was the same. One day when I came back from work, my mother had a message for me. She got me suspicious when she asked me to sit down first. I sat down and held my breath... What does she have to say? Could that be something good? I stared at her face, trying to read her lips...She noticed my nervousness and said,

"Don't worry, son. Everything that happens - happens for better if you believe in God. I hope that you have learned to trust God, since your own efforts didn't work out the way you expected. Believe me, trust God and He will renew your life!"

She paused...and then continued,

"Your wife just got married with the other man."

"How could that be!" I exclaimed. "I never gave her a letter of divorce!"

"Well, it's possible," she replied. "She could have done it in her home country!" "Probably that's what she did," I agreed.

Then I was trying to unfold everything that happened between us. When we got married, she didn't have a green card. She simply used me to get that green card! It was really cruel from her side, how could she mess up my life just because of one piece of the document that she needed?

I called her later and asked, "How could you get married without divorcing me?" "Oh, I forgot to tell you that I took care of that on my own, I just didn't want to bother you."

"Bother me? You took care of that? How could you do that without consulting with me? Besides, where is the divorce license, how come I didn't get a copy?"

Several weeks later I received a copy of my divorce license. It was accurately prepared by her home country authorities and signed by her and someone else in the place of me. I started to understand why God didn't want me to have life together with this tricky liar, who tricked not only me, but also the government, presenting someone else under my identity.

My life went back to a single man style. Actually, it differed from single people's lifestyles because of the label that I had: "DIVORCED". I couldn't believe that this strange woman messed up my life and reputation without any fault from my side! Praise God that my depression didn't throw me into a stage of smoking or drinking, or even something worse...I was trying to keep a decent lifestyle and was getting closer to God. The only things that I couldn't give up yet were sex and parties.

After a little while I met another girl - Belanesh. She lived in one bedroom apartment and soon I moved in with her. She was in love with me and before I knew she started to pressure me into a marriage. I couldn't think about any marriage, because my wounds were too fresh. I didn't know how long would it take for my heart to heal, but I was NOT ready for another commitment. I was trying to put the pieces of my broken life back together. However, she was insisting on getting a promise from me to marry her. In such cases I tried to change the subject. Soon she started visiting the psychic, who could read her hand. One day she went to the psychic and asked her a question about me.

"I would like to know my boyfriend's future," she said.

"All right," psychic replied and took her hand. "Oh, I don't think that you would be pleased with what I saw," she said.

"What did you see?" Belanesh asked anxiously.

"I saw your boyfriend with a white lady, not with you."

When she told me about it, I laughed. It sounded so ridiculous, because I didn't know any white women at that time. She didn't believe me, she was just bugging me to tell her who was that white woman. She called me unfaithful

Journey Through Life

and dishonest. "Don't you see how faithful I am to you? Why don't you believe me?" I said. We argued the whole afternoon until dark, but she was not convinced in the truthfulness of my words.

I went to bed in a disturbed mood. In the middle of the night I heard a voice calling my name. I woke up and said to myself, "Who could call my name at this time of the night?" The voice started to talk within me and I could hear it so clear. I looked around; Belanesh was in a deep sleep. The voice continued talking to me, asking why was I there and why was I putting myself in another mess. I felt that God was talking to me again, urging me to leave that place. Probably, God wanted to get my attention again. I started to believe that he loved me and didn't want me to get hurt another time. He must of knew my sufferings and heard my cry and wanted to show me better way of living. Could be that He wanted to replace my tears with a smile and to heal my broken heart, but I was still wandering like a lost sheep, unaware of the dangers that were surrounding me.

I learned my hard lesson from my own mistakes and I wasn't going to repeat them again. This time I listened to the voice that spoke to me that night and started to pray. I told God that my flesh was so weak, but I was willing to make my first step towards Him. I told Him that I was going to pack my bags and leave this apartment that coming morning. I also asked God to help me straight out my ways in future. "God, if I have to meet someone in the future, let it be a Christian lady so she could help me focus on you in everything I do."

In the morning while Belanesh was out, I did exactly what I promised to God. I packed all my belongings and placed them in the car. Then I waited until she came back home to tell her that I was living. I was waiting for a while, trying to imagine how will she take my final words that I prepared to say. It was really long waiting... I was looking at the clock, but its hands wouldn't move, it felt that the time froze. Few hours lasted as long as eternity.

Finally I heard someone's footsteps, it was Belanesh. She looked at me suspiciously; she felt that something was not right. "Is everything all right?" she asked. I didn't reply to her, I was still in my deep thoughts. And after few moments I said, "Belanesh, please sit down, I would like to talk to you." She looked at me with intently wide opened eyes, and then slowly pulled the chair and sat next to me. Her eyes were fixed on my face with some kind of surprise in them. She drilled me with two brown circular eyes and I started to feel uncomfortable. "Wow, her eyes are really beautiful," I said to myself, but I didn't let the hesitation sneak into my heart. I was firmly assured that my place wasn't here. "I cannot disobey God again," I thought, "this could be my last chance to fix my past. I have to do it!"

"Belanesh, listen to me, please," I continued with the firmness in my voice. "Please don't be mad at me after what I have to say." She sat still, quietly listening to every word I said. "I made a decision this morning that I have to leave. I am sorry, I didn't mean to hurt you in any way, but I have to be honest with you because you deserved it. God told me to get up and leave this place, because this is not my place. I am sorry. I already packed my stuff and ready to go." After these words Belanesh couldn't say anything. She was trying to catch her breath, like a person that lacked oxygen.

Finally, she made a deep sound, "Oooooooooooh" and laid her head on the table. I heard the sounds of weeping, her head and shoulders were quaking on the table and I knew that she was in pain. I waited for her to stop weeping, I felt deeply sorry for her, but I had to be strong. After some time she finally squeezed few words out her lips,

"Why? Why are you doing this to me?"

"I am so sorry, Belanesh, but God is accusing me in living an unrighteous life. I cannot possibly live with any

Journey Through Life

woman without marriage, I feel as guilty as sin. Moreover, I cannot commit myself to a marriage yet, my wounds from my divorce still hurt. I wish that one day you would come to God too."

After these words I left. I couldn't understand my feelings at that time. I didn't know if I was sad or happy about my decision, but I knew one thing that I made the right choice. I started to build faith and knew that God would take care of my future.

I moved back to my mother's house and she was very happy that I came. "I am so happy that you are back in my house," she told me. "You can stay here as long as you wish. Just relax and sort your life out." Mommy will always be mommy, no matter what we do in our lives. No one will ever replace mothers and you will never find a greater love than mother's love, although I found out later that there is a greater love and this is the love of God. God's love could not be compared with any human love or any other kind of love, because God's love is THE GREATEST LOVE. The Bible tells us that GOD is LOVE! I also found out that I didn't need to do anything to obtain that love, because God loved me before I was born. I just needed to believe in Him… All these I found out later…

Meanwhile, I was settling down in my mother's house. I decided to stay in the basement, plus I started to reconstruct it and turned it into one bedroom apartment. During my residence in my mother's house Belanesh still called me to see if I told her the truth. I guess, she still hoped that I would come back…But I made myself busy with home improvement trying to forget my emotional wounds. I kind of put my personal life on hold and it worked for me.

I quit my job for another job in a very large automotive corporation for better pay. The company was rebuilding auto parts and had different plants around the city. However, as soon as I got hired there, I got frustrated with my job, I didn't like it a bit. On the fifth day I decided to quit. I stayed home one day, but someone called me from the Human Resources and asked what happened.

"I am allergic to one of the chemical ingredients that you are using for the parts," I said. "Sorry, but this job is not for me." But he didn't want to let me go.

"Why don't you come back on Monday," he said. "We will let you try something else."

I was amazed to see how they cared about people. I decided to go back and see if I would get any better luck this time. I was given a different job, but it wasn't better than the first one. I didn't want to bother talking to anyone and just didn't show up again. Could you believe that they call me back again? They still wanted me to come back? "Maybe God wanted me to keep this job?" I said and went back. This time they brought me to a different plant and I liked it much better. I decided to stay for a while and see what is in it for me; so I took it more seriously this time. I started to work with a positive attitude. Every day I was getting more comfortable with the job that I was doing and after a month I exceeded everyone's expectations. I was one of the leading quota busters in the whole department. "Well, maybe God really prepared this place for me," I thought. After all these painful months I finally was satisfied with how my life was turning. My new supervisor was a lady; she seemed to be very nice. I liked my department, I had really good co-workers and a nice boss," Alix stopped his story and looked at me with a puzzled smile.

"Who was your supervisor, do I know her," I disturbed Alix's story.

"I will give you two minutes to guess," he said.

I was puzzled. Was he talking about me?

"Please don't test my curiosity, tell me!"

"Well, she is the person that I am talking to now..."

"Really? Thanks for the compliments!"

Journey Through Life

"Guess what! Something else was catching my attention and that was the fragrance that you were wearing."

"Ha-ha-ha," I started to laugh. "So it wasn't me but my perfume that got you attention?"

"Well, actually your perfume coordinated my attention in the right direction. I am this type of person that loves perfumes and colognes very much. I would breathe it in every time you passed by; I was just taking a ride on smelling free perfume. Soon I would recognize that you were near just by the smell without looking." "You did? I had no idea of what was going through your head while I was doing my job. Thanks for revealing that to me."

"How about your Florida vacation and the pictures that you showed to everybody? Remember that you came to me and said that you met with a lot of French speaking people there? I gave you my comments. "If you take me with you next time," I said, "I will interpret for you." You did not seem to be upset at my response."

"You were joking, were you?" I looked at Alix's face, he looked kind of embarrassed, and I almost could see a blush on his face, although it was dark.

It was getting late and I told Alix that we had to go home because my parents would be concerned about me. I thanked him for being open and sincere with me. I really enjoyed his story and his company. He was a real gentleman and since I knew him he always behaved decently, as a true friend. He asked me if we could meet another time to finish this conversation and I said, "All right. Why don't we meet on Saturday?" We drove back home silently, digesting all the information that we learned about each other. Soon I was home. I shook his hand "Good-bye" and ran up the steps of my house. I turned my head back and stopped for a second until his car faded away in the depth of the night.

XXX.   Memories of the Past

After that heart-to-heart conversation with Alix I was trying to understand where I was in this relationship? For sure, Alix became my dear friend. He had that great ability to listen and understand me. I thought that he could be a great counselor, he just had that gift of almost reading people's minds. He could lighten up the person's burden and breathe an inspiration into a broken heart. This was very important to my emotional and sensitive nature. But was there more than just a friendship between us? I was making all kind of analysis on everything that happened so far. Could Alix be my other half that I was looking for or this was just another relationship that never meant to be? I didn't want to put my hopes high, because I had an experience of relationships that never continued…

Slavik was my first love… If I could call it love… It was probably just my child's immature passion…I would blush to the roots of my hair every time I saw him. He noticed that and started to look at me every time I was passing by. I was very young then, about thirteen years old. He lived in my neighborhood. I always stared in the window when he was walking back from school, because he had to pass by my house. One day he met me on the street when I was coming back home from the grocery store.

"Hi, pretty girl," he said. I smiled back and blushed again. One day he invited me to the movie, but I said, "No". I knew that there was a huge separation between us. I was a Christian, he was not. He was just a regular boy that didn't believe in any God. At my young age I already knew that this was not going to work, because I didn't want to cross the line that would separate me from God.

I had many friends that passed by in my life, but I never let anyone get close to me, until I knew that he was the one from God. Another reason that was stopping me from making serious relationships was my goal of immigration. I believed that one day God will open the iron curtain and we will be free to leave that evil-based country. I held myself very tight from sliding down into any emotional hole. I had a very strong self-control. No matter how deep my feelings would be for the person, I would always find strength to pull myself out and walk away. And then I would work on my broken feelings until the wound was healed.

I met Nick in the city where I went to school for fashion design. My girlfriend brought me to her church; actually, it was a youth prayer meeting. I was asked if I wanted to pray aloud and I said, "Yes". I remember that I held a very sincere prayer, even to the tears in my eyes. After the meeting a young man came to me and introduced himself. He was tall and very handsome, his name was Nick. He was an assistant youth pastor in that church. We held a pleasant conversation and I gave him some information about myself: the school I was going to and the church that I was attending. Nick told me that he was glad to meet me and we said "good-bye" to each other.

A few days later I was standing on the bus stop and waiting for the bus that was suppose to bring me to school. I watched the traffic trying to forecast the frequency of the buses that were running in both directions. Then I heard the sound of a motorcycle that was coming closer and closer. I wished that I had one myself, I wouldn't have to wait for the bus. And then I noticed that the motorcycle slowed down as it was getting closer to the bus stop. This got my attention and I looked at the rider that was firmly sitting on the top of the two-wheeler. He stopped right in front of me and looked straight into my face. I will never forget that look. He was looking at me with his drilling eyes like he wanted to break through into my soul. There was so much love in that look that I got embarrassed. Was that a love from the first sight? No, this was the love from the second sight, because I already met him in the prayer meeting, this was Nick.

"Hi, Nick, how are you?" I asked.

"I am fine," he said. "I am on my way to work."

"And I am going to school," I said. "Have a wonderful day." I went to school but those two burning eyes followed me as a shadow for few weeks.

It was Sunday morning and I was ready for my church service. My landlord Maria and I used to go to the same church, we made a great team together. She enjoyed my company and I enjoyed hers. We never missed any church services, in an underground church. We always had to meet in the different places and it was always in someone's house. We were used to the crowded services but we always had a great hospitality. That week Sunday service was scheduled somewhere outside the city; we needed to change bus three times in order to get there. I liked being in church and liked to be there in time. The service started. We sang a few songs, then some of the youth members said poems. After another song and a prayer the pastor got up and started his message. That was the message that we really needed to hear.

"I am going to tell you that you are not alone in suffering persecution from our ungodly government," he said. "There are many other nations that bare the same cross as we are. This person's testimony is a true story and I want you to hear what I have to say. This will give you an encouragement to continue your journey among the surrounding evil. This story is about one Cuban doctor. Cuba, the daughter of Communist system, has a similar political structure as Russia. Therefore, Cuban Christians experienced the same religious persecution and problems as Russian Christians.

This story is about the doctor, who was not a believer. He was a talented and a respected doctor and saved a lot of lives by finding cures for his patients. One day he woke up with a feeling that God talked to him in his dream. "You

Journey Through Life

worked hard saving people's lives, now I want you to start saving souls. Don't be afraid, I will be with you. Today you are going to start ordering and distributing Bibles for Me. I will be guarding you everywhere on your way."

The doctor became fearful. He heard this overpowered voice talking to him and there was nobody, but himself in the room. The more he thought about that, the more he realized that it wasn't just the play of his mind. He felt that the voice was real. He put his hands on his face and fell face down on the floor. He heard the loud beating of his heart and every muscle of his body was trembling.

"I will do anything that You want me to do, just don't leave me, please," he prayed.

After that everything became quiet. He didn't remember how long he spent lying on the floor, but then the buzzing fly landed on his ear and that made him get up on his feet.

As I said earlier, Cuba is one of the countries that adopted the communist ideology. Cubans experienced the same cruel regime, as we experience in the Soviet Union. It wasn't easy to preach the gospel without being persecuted but the doctor didn't think twice. He remembered one of his patients David who was telling him about God. Before he didn't want to believe in any of the "nonsense stories about God". Then he thought that his patient was just delirious from his surgery when he heard him talking about God.

This morning he pulled out his phone directory and looked at the long list of his patients' addresses. He finally spotted the one that he was looking for. "Here it is, David, my strange patient." The doctor called David immediately, but nobody would answer. "I have to find him, I have to!" He called him every hour until finally someone picked up the phone on the other end. "Hi, David, is that you? I've been calling you whole day..." David was a little surprised to hear from his doctor.

"Do you have bad news to tell me?" he asked.

"No, just good ones," doctor replied.

David was very excited to hear about his doctor experience and decided to help him. Soon they found a source where they could purchase Bibles. The doctor started his mission. First he brought a few of them to the office and offered them to his co-workers. A few days later he went to the downtown of Havana where he could find a lot of people on the streets. He found the corner with the biggest flow of pedestrians and started to offer Bibles to everybody who was passing by. The day was finished successfully and the doctor thanked God for this great beginning of his new ministry. He started to feel joy of accomplishing something for God. On the following day doctor went to his spot carrying even more Bibles. He wanted to achieve even greater success than he did yesterday. However, at the moment he arrived he was arrested. His charge was distribution of illegal materials. He was taken to the Cuban authorities for questioning. Since Cuba was a Communist country where Christianity was forbidden, the doctor was found guilty and was sentenced to imprisonment. In spite of all the trials he had to get through, he did everything with joy because Jesus lived in his heart. Conditions in Cuban prisons are terrible. Prison authorities applied a lot of cruel tools and tortures to break prisoners' spirit, especially Christian prisoners.

An extremely "hot" plan was created for the doctor. A few guards grabbed the doctor's arms and pushed him out of his cell. They commanded him to follow them. He was brought to a "special" cell, chained to a chair and placed under a drop of water. He didn't remember, how long it lasted, a day or longer, but he gave himself into Jesus hands and didn't even feel anything but the sound of the drop. Since that attempt didn't change his mind about God, the "adventures" continued...

He was placed in an extremely freezing room wearing only one thin T-shirt. From the freezing room he was moved

Journey Through Life

to an extremely heated room, back and forth... After a week of these non-human tortures they expected the doctor to fall on his knees and beg for mercy. They miscalculated his spiritual strength because they didn't know that God was with him throughout his tortures. He was completely exhausted, but didn't have any bitterness in his heart. He was joyful and loving as always before. After they couldn't get anything out of this man, except the love of Christ, the furious officers threw him back into one of the cells. While he was lying on the floor, something was telling him that he was not alone. He slowly got up and looked around. Wow! He had company! A huge brown bear was staring at him from the corner of the cell. The doctor froze in one pose, trying to predict the bear's next move! The bear was looking at him for quite a while but then it didn't find anything attractive in the doctor. After a couple of minutes, it put its head down, yawn a few times and settled itself for a nap. The officers became malicious! "What is happening with this man? Is he a human or a ghost?" They didn't know that the Holy Ghost was with him all that time. Without getting any "success", they dragged him to another cell and left him alone.

One of the Christian organizations learned about the doctor, whose faith in God couldn't be broken by all the demonic powers of Cuba, and decided to find a way to bring him to the US. After some time the Cuban government released him to the US authorities where he found a refuge and peace."

I was so absorbed by the pastor's message that I didn't pay attention to anything else that was going on in that house. The story sounded so similar to the story of my father that I would never forget it. The pastor finished his sermon and after the final prayer the service was over. I got up from the chair and turned around searching with my eyes for Maria. Suddenly, my eyes fell on the face that was so familiar to me. Nick?! What was he doing there? He never came to this church before! He was talking to someone and they both were looking around... I knew that he was searching for me...Oh, no! I was not ready for that! Not quite yet! I reacted very fast. With the increasing heartbeats I made a few steps away and hid in the bathroom. "O, God, please help me," I said. "If this is not the one that You have chosen for me, please help me handle my emotions and don't let me get embarrassed in front of the whole church."

In a few minutes I cooled down and slowly walked out of the bathroom. Half of the people already left and Nick wasn't there any more. "Galina, where were you, I thought that you left with the youth?" it was Maria's soft voice, who was still chatting with the owner of the house. I looked at her face to see if she had any clue about Nick's visit, but she didn't seem to notice anything. "Praise God", I said and we went home.

My school was over and after the graduation I got my certificate and moved back to my hometown. I missed my parents and siblings but I gained a great experience on how to make a living away from home. This was the first time I spent a year on my own and I thought that I did great. When I returned I was more maturer and could even give advice to my younger sisters and brother.

Our local church was really small and we traveled a lot, visiting other nearby churches. There was a convention coming to the church that was located in the nearby town Suhoe. We liked conventions because we loved to meet with Christians from other areas. My whole family went to the convention. We met many people and took many pictures for the memory of that event. Could you imagine; I ran into Nick once again! "Nick, how did you get here?" I asked. My voice trembled. "I simply asked your girlfriend where you came from and then I found out about this convention," he said. Oh, no... I was puzzled. Did God send him on my way? Could this be God's purpose? I wasn't getting it... I liked

Journey Through Life

Nick, who wouldn't? But for some reason I had a feeling that he was not the right person for me. Nick noticed my confusion and, I guess, he didn't want to make any scenes in front of my family that was standing right behind me. "Let's catch up with the convention," he said and then added, "I will talk to you when it's over. Okay?" I mumbled something uncertain and we moved toward the house of worship. That day we left convention early and I never saw Nick again.

All these memories were like the heavy clouds in my head and I wasn't sure what direction my life was going to take at this time. Perhaps, Alix was my destiny, but I simply didn't know. It was a long day and I was feeling very tired. I knelt down and expressed all my concerns to the Lord. I knew that He would put all pieces of the puzzle together.

XXXI. My Life Is Making An Amazing Turn

It was Friday afternoon when I waited for Alix to come out from the building. "I see that you are in a hurry. Are we still meeting on Saturday?" he asked. "Of course," I said, "let's do that."

We met again. It was early Saturday morning, when we were sitting on the bench of downtown Philadelphia. I enjoyed the view of Franklin Institute Museum. The fountain at the entrance of museum was throwing large streams of water in the air, that was breaking into thousands drops when was falling back down. Some of the drops were reaching the bench where we sat and I enjoyed the feeling of fresh greeting from the fountain that was saying "Hello" to us. We sat quietly for a while, enjoying the views of awakening city. I recalled our last meeting in the park and my conversation with Alix. He bears a lot of pain from his relationships. How could people be so cruel? They walked far away from the purpose that they were created for. There is so much evil in this world and instead of striving for "good", people implement more "evil". Praise God that He sent His son Jesus to this world to take our sins, what would we do if He didn't? We would have to be perished with our sins forever…Jesus is the only island where we can find safety and peace and the eternal life. Praise the Lord!

I started the conversation. "Listen," I said. "I enjoyed your story very much and thought about it a lot. I think, that God let all this turmoil happen in your life to get your attention. Sometimes problems push us to search for God; otherwise we would not look for Him. And when we look for Him, things that we consider bad He changes for good if we trust in Him. Apostle Paul said in Romans 8:28, "We know that in everything God works for the good of those who love Him." I already told you that I was born in The Soviet Union, where Christianity was totally persecuted, and how much efforts I had to put to continue loving and worshiping God. At the same time I found out how much Jesus loved me and helped me to accomplish many great things in my life. I wouldn't have done anything without His powerful hand guiding and supporting me in all my ways. He always sent His angels to protect me from the fire in the middle of a burning oven. I walked on the top of the blades but never got a scratch. KGB officers held me for a day, but they had to let me go, because God commanded them to. They worshipped evil but obeyed God without realizing that. When it comes to protect His servants God will use anything or anyone to do that, because He is all-powerful creator of the Universe."

Alix gave me his full attention, I thought that he enjoyed listening to me. Our conversation would go for hours and we seemed to share our internal worlds. We both learned from each other so much that we wished that these "sessions" never stopped. I felt very conformable in Alix's company, maybe because he was a good listener, or maybe for some other reason. We met frequently and we always had more and more to share with each other. I talked to him about Jesus and my personal experiences and I felt that my story didn't have an ending. He told me that he enjoyed listening to me all the time.

After a few months of friendship we met in our most favorite place. It was one of the oldest Philadelphia parks.

"What a great place to relax and enjoy the nature!" I proclaimed and looked at Alix. He didn't seem to hear my comments; he was just staring at one point on the top of a tree.

"Is everything all right?" I asked him, because I knew that something was bothering him. He took some time to answer me; it seemed like he was preparing a confession to say. I gave him a few minutes to think over whatever he was preparing to say. I couldn't push him, I had to wait for the right moment. Then he started to talk and I felt that it was something important.

"God was trying to worn me about that marriage," he said, "but I disobeyed Him and got the punishment that I deserved. Why was I so blind?" He stopped at that point. There was so much regret in his voice that I had a pity for him. I knew that he was waiting for my feedback.

"God can fix anything that is broken, it doesn't matter how much damage was done. Jesus loves us all, you just have to go to Him and confess your sin. He will forgive you and will give you a new start in your life." I showed him a passage in the Bible – I Corinthians 7, verse 15, that says, "But if those who are not believers decide to leave, let them leave. When this happens, the Christian man or woman is free." "This verse is about married couples, and I hope that you understood the meaning of this verse. That's O.K that your ex-wife left you; let her leave. If Bible says that you are free, you are free indeed, no matter what happened in your past."

Alix looked at me with some kind of amusement in his eyes; it's like I showed him a great discovery!

"Is that right?" he asked.

"Here it is, written black on white in God's Word." He looked in my Bible to make sure that the words were there.

"Praise the Lord!" he proclaimed. "You don't know what you just did for me! You just healed my wounds! I knew that we met for a reason! I remember when Belanesh came from psychic and psychic told her that I would be with the white woman. I don't believe in psychic reading, but the Bible teaches us that God could use anything or anybody to get our attention."

"That's true," I said. "In one of the books of the Bible – Numbers 22, verse 28 says that God made donkey to talk to Balaam to get his attention. God is the author of the whole

Journey Through Life

Universe, He is THE BEGINNING and THE END, and nothing is impossible for God."

Alix revived! His face was shining like he just saw a miracle. Then he dipped his hand in one of his pockets and pulled out a little box. He knelt down on one knee in front of me and presented me with that tiny box. First I couldn't figure out what he was doing.

"Come on", I said. "Are you playing a Romeo today or what?"

Then I realized that he was very serious. "It cannot be", I whispered and stretched out my shaken arm towards the box. I was trying to say something but I couldn't find words. I felt like a cold wind got through my whole body and I turned into a statue. When the first shock went away, I asked quietly, "What is it?"

"Please open it," Alix said. He was looking at me with his wide opened eyes, studying my face. There was a little fear in his look mixed with hesitation. When I opened the box, a little beautiful eye of diamond sparkled in my face. It held the play of lights in it. I never saw anything beautiful like this. It was a marvelous, very feminine engagement ring.

"Please say, "Yes," Alix's voice was trembling. I felt like a hot wave hit my face and it turned red. I was trying to catch my breath. After a minute of silence I asked him what made him think that I was the right person for him? He told me that he had feelings for me for a while and they were growing stronger and stronger. One day when he asked me about my personal life I told him that I never knew any man in my entire life. It was astonishing for him to hear that the young woman in my age (I was thirty-one) never dated any guy. He said that at this time it was very hard to find somebody who didn't get involved with the other person. "All these details just reinforced my decision of proposing to you." He looked in my eyes again. I could see the fear mixed with hope written all over his face. The sound of his voice left an echo in my ears "Please say "Yes...yes...yes..."

"I would love to be your wife, Alix, if God agrees with it. But first I have to spend some time in prayers and get an answer from Him. I always asked for God's directions in my life. Marriage is one of the major events in person's life. I cannot take it lightly. I would like to get married and have a family, but before I take a vow, I have to ask God, I cannot do it on my own."

"Oh, thank you," he whispered. "I love you very much!"

"I love you too," I said. "Let's just see what the Lord has to say." He seemed to be happy with my answer, although, it wasn't certain.

"Let's pray now," he said. We bowed our heads together and prayed.

Since that day Alix started to see life in a different dimension. He was getting closer to God and he finally understood everything that his aunt told him earlier. God really had a different plan for him.

XXXII. Reaction of My Family

One day my mother found my pictures taken with Alix in Long Wood Garden, Pennsylvania. She asked me if that was my friend and I said, "Yes." My mother was very surprised! Actually, "surprised" wouldn't be the right word to describe my mother's reaction. She was devastated! How could she accept the idea of her lovely daughter being with someone with totally opposite parameters: nationality, culture, language, he might not be a believer, as my mother would like to see her future son-in-law. I was trying to convince her that Alix was such a nice and polite gentleman, that she shouldn't worry about him. "He is a born again Christian, what else could you expect from the person, mom?" I said. "Didn't you teach me to look at the inner beauty of a person, because the outer look could be deceiving? But Alix has both: as much as he is handsome and kind. And I know that he loves God with all his heart." Then I added,

"Mom, please don't be shocked, but that young man asked me to marry him. I didn't say anything to him yet. Mommy, help me make a decision, please."

Although my mother was devastated; she handled it right She only said to me,

"I wasn't aware that you had such a serious friendship with someone, but that's O.K. I cannot argue with you, Galina, you could be right. God sees the person's heart better than we do, so I am going to pray and seek for an answer from God."

My mother prayed and fasted on her own because she wanted to make sure that I made the right choice. I didn't argue, because I knew how right she was. With all the love for God that I had and the respect for my mother I patiently waited for an answer. Meanwhile, my mother went to visit a Slavic church in Massachusetts. At a prayer meeting there she asked to pray for me in an unspoken request. After the prayer meeting someone approached my mother. "Sister, are you the one that had an unspoken request at the prayer meeting?" "Yes," my mother replied. "I have a revelation from God for you. Why are you doubting in your daughter's choice and why are you fighting with this idea in your heart? Stop fighting and accept the person that your daughter chose, because this is God's will. God sent this person for your daughter and is going to bless them. And now... go home and tell your daughter about this revelation."

My mother was stunned when she heard this response. From that very moment all her doubts disappeared, like night shadows dissolve at the first sunray. Strengthened and encouraged by these words, my mother felt like a burden fell off her shoulders. It was such a proper and beautiful response from God! She came home on the following day with a very wide smile on her face.

"Come here, Galina. I need to tell you a secret, secret from God." I couldn't wait to hear what was she going to tell me.

"What is it? What is it? Please tell me, because I am loosing my patience."

"All right," she said. And she repeated all the "golden" words, which she heard in Massachusetts.

"Praise God!" I screamed. "I had a feeling that he was my other half! Praise God! Alleluia!"

I was convinced that I was on the right track. It became clear to all of us – we had to start preparing for the big day. I was very excited and couldn't wait for our marriage to actually take place. My family and I praised and glorified God.

Here came the time for me to introduce Alix to my parents and the family. "Guess, who is coming for dinner," I said to my mother. "It's my dearest friend Alix." When he came to my house, everyone was surprised to see him. We were from Ukraine, he was from the Caribbean. But in spite of being a complete stranger to my folks, they welcomed him very well. They all knew God's response about this relationship and they couldn't say anything else. In my family God's word was the last word and Alix respected that very much.

XXXIII. Rejected by the Church

My family was helping and supporting me all the way until my wedding day. However, I had to meet with a big opposition from my church and the pastor. As soon as people from my community learned about our engagement, they started to bring all kind of gossip about us. They made up their own stories and wanted others to believe them. They pulled all the efforts to break this marriage. Afterwards, two of the major Slavic churches attempted to boycott and ruin my wedding completely. Under all this pressure, I had to go on against the stream. This was a real test for me: sink or swim! I was absolutely drained under the maximum physical and mental pressure. Some days I didn't know how to make it to the other day. Physical work was already taking most of my strength. Evening classes in the College were adding pressure to my overwhelmed schedule. The only hours that I had left for homework and for the wedding preparations were late night hours and weekends. I had to do everything on my own. I spent many nights making my wedding gown and the dresses for the bridesmaids. Reservations, invitations, decorations, menu arrangements... I was overwhelmed! "Galina, did you order cake yet? How about the reception hall decoration is it taken care of? Wow, you forgot to invite one of the church friends..." I was a wedding planner, wedding organizer, dressmaker, invitation distributor and the bride-to-be at the same time. On the top of everything I had to resist the pressure that was building up against me. People didn't want to hear anything about God's revelation; neither did they want to accept this man in my community. The Pastor of my church with his wife and the daughter initiated this entire bustle around my wedding.

"Think about how your children are going to come out of this mixed race," pastor's wife was trying to persuade me in the correctness of her words. I couldn't believe my ears

Journey Through Life

that I heard such words from the lips of the pastor's wife! Was that really a Christian church or was it just acting one? They sounded more like undercover Hollywood to me. I was thankful to God that He gave me strength to handle that trial. I was confident in doing the right thing and knew that God would help me to resist all the attacks of Slavic community.

Many nights I cried in my pillow, I had to change my pillowcases all the time. I was depressed and lost my appetite. Some days I couldn't stand up without holding on to a chair or something else, the world would be spinning in front of my eyes. My body was exhausted; I was counting days before the wedding.

My mother started to worry about me and asked all her friends to pray about this situation. But everywhere she went she got the same answer from God, as the first one. I couldn't go back to my church because my pastor and the majority of the members decided to exclude me from the church members, just because I was marrying Alix. I thought that church was the place with open doors for everyone, therefore, I was disappointed in this one.

In the middle of the on-going straggles of this difficult period in my life, I was invited to visit one small church in Lancaster, Pennsylvania. We had a wonderful worship there. In the prayer I let all of my tears out, I couldn't hold them any more. As many times before, I felt so helpless in front of the merciless cruelty that was surrounding me and didn't know how to take it anymore. Being crushed to the ground, I thought that the life was running out of my feet. I just wanted to detach myself from reality and fly far away, where my enemies would not catch up with me where I could hear beautiful heavenly songs. I cried and asked God to take me home, to heaven, where there will be no tears, no pain, no sadness, no death, but happiness and joy forever. Anyway, what was the purpose of living, if suffering had to take place of happiness and human cruelty invaded the peace in human hearts?

"I know that you are hurt and I know that you are asking God to take you home, but this is not your time yet," with this words someone touched my arm. I opened my eyes and looked at the lady that was talking to me. She continued, "You will get through this pain and problems and you will find joy in your life. God cannot take you to heaven now, because you have a lot of work to do for God. You will be working with "those" people and God will use you a lot. And right now wipe off your tears and put yourself together, because God wants you to be a strong soldier in the army of Christ!"

The voice of the lady stopped. I was trying to wipe off the tears, but instead, there were two rivers running down from my face. This time they were the tears of joy! I didn't know how the lady could read my heart, it could only be if God revealed it to her. God revealed her the state of my mind and gave her an answer for me. There was not even one person that knew what I was thinking about and what I was praying for. This was the message from God! After that prayer I grew the wings of faith and hope. My pressure went down after that day and God gave me strength to continue preparations for my wedding day. God supported me and strengthened me in many different ways at that time. If it wasn't for God, I would probably die. But then, I didn't want to die any more, I wanted to worship and glorify God as long as I lived with all my strength and with all my heart.

There was another message from the same Lancaster lady for me, this time it was in her dream. A prophet approached her when she slept and said, "Galina is getting married with a man of color." That was it. That was a short message in her short dream. She didn't understand the message, but she knew that the message was for me. When she called me, I made it clear to her,

"Yes that's right! My fiancé is a man of color. I cannot hide any secrets from you any more!"

She laughed,

"Isn't God amazing?"

"Yes, He is," I said. "And praise be to him forever!"

She was surprised and, at the same time, happy for me. She was very supportive and gave me an advice to be strong, because people cannot destroy what God is doing. I received a lot of support and encouragement from Christians that really loved God and lived by His word. In the middle of the storm I found a beautiful circle of friends. I thanked God again and again for answers to my prayers. I really needed it! Although I was all exhausted physically and mentally, but I believed that God brought Alix and I together, so I never gave up. I heard many revelations and knew that I was serving a big God, who will help me get through any people-created mess.

XXXIV. The Big Wedding Day

With God's help I made it to my wedding day. Chaplain Loni from my job told me later, "I was watching you throughout the time of your wedding preparations. I knew all the problems and difficulties that you had to go through and I really thought that you wouldn't make it. I realized how strong you had to be in order to deal with all the mess that people purposely created for you." "Actually, it wasn't my strength, Jesus handled everything for me," I replied.

Meanwhile, the wedding day approached… After three to four hours of sleep that I had that night, I was getting ready for my "big day". I lost "every gram of fat" from my body; my weight was one hundred and three pounds. My sister Dina was my beautician. She had to put my hair up to make it a base for my crown. My other two sisters were busy dressing up themselves, because they were my bridesmaids. Once in a while one of them would throw a joke at me.

"What is happening to you these days? I never saw you dried up so much like this time. Was that the love that dried you to the bones? You look like a witch, you just missing a broom," Dina laughed.

I was trying to smile, but the smile looked crooked on my bony face. My face was pale, there was not even a shadow of blush on it. My nose stretched out and looked longer than usually. I needed a lot of makeover to get somewhat a decent look for the wedding. I prayed that God gave me strength to cross this tough intersection of my life.

A limousine arrived soon. Carrying heavy dress and the crown, I slowly walked down the steps, holding on to the railing. I felt like an ancient overdressed statue. The bridesmaids and I got into the limo and started on our way to the church. In the church I saw few people that were already waiting for me. The owner of my company where I worked came by to give me his best wishes. He had to leave

Journey Through Life

soon prior to the beginning of the ceremony. I was stuck in a dressing room waiting for the moment of "walking down the aisle". The minute hand of the church wall clock wouldn't move. Did they glue it to the face of the clock? Perhaps, I was too anxious to get over with all this "ceremonial stuff". I stood at the corner of the room watching the human traffic moving back and forth, in and out. Could somebody tell me when it was my turn to walk into the sanctuary? Instead, I was told out that there was a delay.

"What happened?" I asked.

My father went out somewhere to take care of the drinks for my reception.

"Wow! Why in the world did he do that?"

Nothing was going as planned. I sent one of my guests to my house to find and bring my father back to the church... The ceremony was delayed for about two hours, and finally my father arrived... This gave me some relief, but then I was told about another delay! The best man went back to his home to pick up his camcorder that he forgot to take with him in the first place. Could you believe all these were happening on my wedding day? I was getting more and more nervous. If I could measure the level of my frustration, it would probably be out off the scale.

"Oh, Jesus! Why are all these things happening to me? I never saw such a disorganized wedding! Oh, help me, please."

The piano player came up to me, trying to cheer me up.

"Well, a bad beginning means good life," she said.

These few words that came from a good heart encouraged me at that moment.

Soon after, the best man came back, the wedding went on. I remember standing in front of Alix and repeating pastor's words, "...for better, for worse..." I really wanted to reverse this traditional speech, and say, "...for worse, for better…" because I thought that I already got all the "worse". When I lifted up my eyes to look at the guests and visitors, I discovered that half of the church was just empty seats.

"What happened?" I was questioning myself. "I invited over three hundred people to my wedding!"

Unable to resolve this puzzle, I just stopped thinking for a moment and concentrated on the voice of the pastor. I prayed for God to send me the answers that I needed. Knowing that I am the child of God, I shouldn't be carrying any worries. Instead I had to build a faith that God would take care of my "today and tomorrow".

Meanwhile, the pastor continued with the ceremony.

"May the groom kiss the bride…" And then he pronounced Alix and I to be "husband and wife". I got a deep breath; I was so glad that the ceremony was over. That was the end of the old chapter of my life and the beginning of the new one. Problems and issues don't leave our lives completely, but God never leaves us unattended while we go through difficult times. He always gives enough strength and support to handle every situation in life.

After the ceremony our friends greeted my new husband and me and we went to the place of reception. A large beautiful hall, decorated with silver and gold flowers, balloons and arches was expecting us at the Ukrainian Cultural center. I was thankful to the band that met us with the best music ever. Things started much better there, I felt a relief. It was too soon to say that the things finally would go smooth. It was also too early to make any conclusions prior to the end of the evening. And BOOM! Soon after my arrival I was told that my wedding host didn't show up. I was not surprised. These kinds of things have been happening to me ever since I decided to get married. I was waiting to see what was going to be next. In a little while my brother-in-law came forward and told me that he could be a host for that evening.

Journey Through Life

"I greatly appreciate that," I said and few tears dropped down of my eyes. Two-thirds of the tables were empty. The missing group was the group that was boycotting me. This was the group of hypocrites that call themselves friends, but at the crucial moment of your life they would be the first ones to strike you from the back. There will always be a Judas around us; we just have to watch out!

The guests filled one-third of the tables, and I realized that I wasn't completely alone. My wonderful God was on my side, my lovely husband was shoulder-to-shoulder with me plus there were one hundred guests who decided to come and share my happiness with me. I thanked each and everyone who came to support me in the time when I desperately needed it.

How about that mad group, that was plotting against me? Why some of our family friends ran away listening to the gossips of the others? The man that I asked to be the host was one of my father's best friends. We prayed and worshipped together, we left my country in the same wagon, and we were just like one family. However, when the time came to show his friendship and support, he appeared to be on the other side. Anyway, how do we recognize real friends? We recognize them at the times of a need…

Later after my wedding Vladimir (the runaway host) came to my father and tried to explain why he did what he did. "It was because the pastor of my church warned me that I would be exhorted from the church if I appeared in your daughter's wedding ceremony even for a moment", he said. He preferred to lose the friendship but to keep his position in church. I was very disappointed to hear such a non-sense excuse. He left that church later anyway…

The wedding was coming to an end, people were giving us their blessings and wishes. I only wanted to get over with everything and relax. Waving "bye" to our guests we left the reception hall.

After that day all my tension was gone. I needed a break in order to go on with my life: my husband and I are the family now. I was trying to forget all the bitterness that was surrounding my wedding. It was not so easy to forgive and forget, but as a Christian, I had to do that. I couldn't clear out those sour memories from my mind for a long time. Every time when I saw someone from my former church, I felt a bitter ball in my throat. I didn't know if I had to make a fake smile or just to pass by without looking. I was puzzled for a while working on the strategies of forgiveness. But God gave me strength to fight with my offended feelings. It was a difficult process, but I was willing to do it, because I love God with all my heart and want to obey His Word.

XXXV. Family Life

After all, the pain that I had to take from people's criticism God replaced with His blessings. God works in mysterious ways in lives of people that trust Him. Alix was thankful that he didn't reject God, although he had fallen many times. Many times, God stretched out His hand and pulled him out of his troubles.

First year of family life was quite an adjustment for Alix and me. We both worked full time and I was taking evening classes in the local Community College. It was a difficult schedule especially when I got pregnant, but I managed it well.

First we lived in my in-law's house; we had a room on the second floor and another room in the basement. Due to the size of my family at that time, we fit there well. Alix's mother is one of the sweetest people that I ever met. She was kind, loving and helpful and I will never regret sharing the same roof with her. Alix's youngest sister Stacey also lived in the same house. We were one happy family. My mother-in-law taught me how to cook Caribbean food. Since Alix loved his traditional food, I tried to satisfy him with my cooking. My efforts paid off – Alix enjoyed my meals so much that he eventually gained a lot of weight.

We all were happy and enjoyed those wonderful moments of our life.

The birth of Alix Jr. brought some excitement and even concerns in my life. As a new mother, I was protective and even a little scared for the baby's well being. Every cry of my son would make me nervous. First few months I ran to the doctor two-three times a week just to make sure that the baby was all right. The doctor would assure me time after time that there was nothing wrong with the baby; some babies just cry more than the others! Crying was the way babies communicate to their mothers. I heard this explanation so many times, but still was staying alert when the junior had to cry longer than I expected. A few factors contributed to my son's fussiness: he was born premature, under weight and on the top of that he was circumcised. I had to give him a lot of attention and care to help him get through the most critical trimester of his life.

I had to stop my education, because my men needed a lot of my attention. Taking advantage of the babysitting service, provided by my family, I continued with my full time job. I adjusted my lifestyle to the working mother's one. I had to get up really early and drop off the baby to the babysitter's house prior to getting to work on time. I just wished that days were longer and nights could have some extra hours. Unable to obtain enough sleep at night I always felt tired. I was afraid of being caught asleep in front of my computer at work, but fortunately, this never happened. My body had no choice but to get adjusted to my new schedule. Soon I handled all the activities the same way I did before, even with less hours of sleep. Alix, Jr. was growing up and the more he grew, the more he looked just like his father. My husband was overwhelmingly happy with his first born son. He told me later, that he was praying during my pregnancy for a son that would look just like him. "All right," I said. "You got what you asked for, and now is my turn. I want to have a daughter."

It didn't take long for my wish to come true; when Alix Jr. turned two, my daughter Taisa was born. My husband and I were even happier about how it turned out... We had two healthy beautiful children, a boy and a girl, what else would a young family wish for? O, yes, there was something else: a house. With the birth of Taisa we started to feel that we needed more space than my mother-in-law could offer us. The search for a house started. Abington Township attracted us more than others; we were also trying to find something affordable. We finally found something that we were looking

Journey Through Life

for. It was a nice lot on a quiet street in Willow Grove with the shell of a burnt house on it. My husband just fell in love with the lot and location. He was visualizing what could he make out of that shell. Being so enthusiastic about rebuilding that house, Alix couldn't wait for the time to start working on it. Although, it required a lot of work, Alix took a goal to turn this house into a palace.

Soon the work started. Not only he planned to rebuild the old house, but also to make an addition to it. It took almost six-years to build the house of our dream. It was a huge six-bedroom house with an apartment on the other side. It had patio, deck, family room with a fireplace in it, playground for the children and much more...

Meanwhile, the construction was in progress... Every night after work, on weekends, during vacation and holidays Alix worked on the house. It was six years of persistent hard work... With the birth of Taisa I was off work for nine months. Alix was the only source of income for the family at the time when we needed a triple income due to the ongoing construction. Moreover, we were still living in my in-law's house... Our financial situation was getting worse and worse. I had no choice, but to go to my piggy-bank reserve. Many times I would walk to the nearest bank with wrapped coins, strolling my infant daughter and holding the hand of my two-year old. Soon I realized that I had no choice, but to ask my mother for a babysitting favor again and to go back to work. With God's help things worked out well: my mother stepped in to help me without any hesitation. My former supervisor offered me my job back. We got back on track and I left my piggy bank for a while...

My husband always wanted to get involved with the church ministry. He is not the kind that comes to church once a week; sits on the bench for a few hours and gets satisfied. My husband loved to take part in the church life; I did too. It was the right time for us to release the pressure that we had building up for a while and to get involved in a ministry. Soon Alix and I started a movie program for the youth. Without wasting any time Alix purchased a projector, Christian videos and all the equipment needed to make the program run. I sewed a movie screen myself out of large pieces of a heavy cotton material.

The pastor of the church was very excited, when he heard about our project. He welcomed our idea and scheduled our program once every other month. The program was our ministry and we were very excited about it. The church benefited from our program spiritually and materially due to our multiple fundraising events that we did.

Unfortunately, after a few years our ministry faded away. The church got overbooked with different programs and events that they couldn't keep us scheduled on a regular basis. We asked God to help us understand why our ministry was coming to an end? But when the time passed by we understood that God was preparing something different for us. We pursued God's will more and more and He led us in the right direction.

XXXVI. All the Troubles Come at Once

Meanwhile, the work on the house continued… Day after day, week after week, month after month and even year after year my husband was working on this huge task of completing the work on the house. The time was running out, so did the money… We found ourselves working hard for the bills. Bills were accumulating so much, that I couldn't stop worrying about all the payments that we had. Elders usually say, "Excessive thinking would not do any good but would age you prematurely." And this is true. The worries would only give me headaches or cause "butterflies in the stomach". There is nothing more you could do than your best. Only God can bypass the earthly laws and create a miracle. He has an exit out of any situation.

With God's help and two incomes we were able to conquer our debts. When my daughter Taisa turned fifteen months old, we moved into the house. At that time we had only one finished bedroom, one bathroom and the kitchen, just enough for us to start up. The rest of the house, including apartment, needed much more work. Well, we were happy that we could move in.

My father and mother couldn't wait for us to finish the apartment: they were planning to sell their house and move in with us as soon as our house was ready. My father was getting anxious and was asking me from time to time: "When will be the big day?" My husband couldn't estimate the time very well due to the shortage of finances needed to complete the work. But he pushed hard and did his best to achieve the goal. Alix hired a few people to speed up the process and to shorten the time. However, he couldn't afford the helpers for too long, he had to continue the work by himself. I could see the progress every week, but the end was not near yet.

Soon after we moved in I got pregnant with my third child. During my pregnancy a lot of things happened to us. This was the longest pregnancy that I ever had! I thought that it lasted an eternity...That year everything worked against us.

My husband had a legal trouble due to the car accident that actually happened two years ago. The persecuting party decided to make a legal case out of the accident and the court was scheduled at the time of my pregnancy. This issue bothered me very much. I had been praying for a while for God to settle it for us. My car broke down; it needed a new engine. My new boss was trying to demote me from my job that I did for years. But the worst of all was the health of my father. He got a stroke and was partially paralyzed on his right side; then, he had two heart attacks. I was completely brokenhearted.

Every single day I asked God why did I have to go through all these trials while I was carrying a new life inside of me? How was it possible to fight with all these problems when I was pregnant with the baby? Could I handle all of these? I wasn't sure! All my inner being was filled with an unspeakable pain. I felt that a part of me was dying every day... I was trapped... My faith was running out... Five years after my wedding and I was stuck again. It was very very difficult to go on from day to day, week to week, dragging a heavy burden inside of me. I didn't know how, but God was giving me strength to handle that.

The first good news came from my boss. She revised her decision and told me, "Galina, since you are pregnant, I will not make any changes in your job. But remember, if it wasn't for your pregnancy, you would be in the factory ground as of today."

Journey Through Life

Have you ever thought of what makes one mad, or angry? Actually, if you ask the mad he wouldn't even know himself. He might try to find a reason, but it wouldn't be the real one. He wouldn't even realize that it comes from the sinful nature that fills the heart with all kinds of evil desires. My boss never liked me for some reason that I never knew. Maybe because she was a woman like me and felt a competition? Anyway, I was happy that God touched my supervisor's heart that she reversed her decision after my intensive prayers.

Two months later Alix's attorney called him with good news, "The persecuting party withdraw their complaint and the accident court was cancelled." This was the second victory over the problems that I had. Jesus removed some of the obstacles from my way and eased up my burden but not for too long.

When you think that you are on your way up, beware, the way out of problems may not be near yet. Day by day my wonderful loving father was getting sicker and sicker. He was transferred from one hospital to another, but there was no sign of improvement. His heart was not functioning right, his conditions worsened. Doctors suggested that he had to go for the heart cauterization procedure – he seemed to be relieved after it was done. Due to the multiple blockages in the main arteries a necessity of a by-pass surgery was inevitable. Being instructed of the risks that the surgery could bring, my father denied it. I became even more concerned about his condition. The only thing that's left for me to do was to pray and hope that he would get better.

One late night when I finished preparing for the following day and fell asleep, the phone rang. I jumped out of the bed, it was 11:30 PM. I was wondering who would call that late? When I picked up the phone, it was my sister Tanya. From her trembling voice I understood that something BAD happened. "Tanya," I asked quickly, "is everything all right?" "No," she responded and got quiet for a moment. I heard her heavy breathing on the other side of the line. Finally she squeezed a few words out of herself, "Our father passed away." "O, Jesus!" I exclaimed and slowly slid down on the bed. "Could that be true? I need my father in my life so much, how could You let this happen?" I touched my face to make sure that I was awake. Oh, no! It wasn't a dream! "Oh, no, no, no..." my voice got stuck in the throat and the sudden fear froze my entire body, that I couldn't move. "Am I turning into a stone?" I was asking myself. I wanted to cry, but I couldn't, I wanted to scream, but I had no sound in my voice, I wanted to pray, but for some reason I didn't know how to do it any more. The only thing that was moving in my body fast was my heart: it was pounding in my chest so heavily, that I was afraid it would wake up everybody in the house. I fell into a deep depression. Deeply in my heart I knew that I had to maintain a healthy and happy lifestyle for the sake of my unborn baby, but I couldn't. I simply didn't know how to help myself. In a state of shock and confusion I froze for many days and nights. I didn't know if there was morning or evening... I forgot if food had a taste. Nothing exited me any more, nothing made sense. The world was covered with a black cloud, so was my heart. I was just a breathing robot who had no heart, no feelings except the burning pain that wouldn't go away. I didn't know how to wake up back to life, neither how to heal my pain.

Weeks after my father's funeral my internal springs finally moved the heavy rock that was pressing my heart and I broke up in tears. I cried and cried and I thought that I would never stop crying. Then I remembered my two little children that needed me so much! I remembered that I carried a new life within me...and my poor husband who ran out of ideas of how to bring me back... Suddenly, I woke up... to life. I realized that there are people that I loved and cared for and they loved me very much. There was a purpose in life. Death is just a temporary separation from the ones you love, but then there will be a magnificent reunion that will last forever! I spent a lot of time in prayers, asking God to forgive me and to protect my fetus from all the hurricanes that entered my life. At that time I was seven months pregnant.

January twenty second, nineteen ninety-seven was my last day of work before I took a maternity leave from my job. My boss never came up or said anything to me about my leave. The only thing she ever asked me during my whole pregnancy was, "How many kids are you planning to have? Ten?" It was a rude question considering that she was a woman herself. Everybody else in my department gave me all kind of blessings and wishes for the new baby. They even made a baby shower and awarded me with presents. This was a completely different atmosphere than the attitude of my rough "boss". With all the farewells I left my working place.

The week that I stopped working, our only car started to give problems. I was concerned of how would I get to the hospital if the car doesn't get fixed. The problem with the car was the radiator, for some reason it wasn't giving any heat, but produced a lot of smoke instead. It was good enough to bring my husband to his job, but I wouldn't travel in it with the baby that was coming any day. How could I bring baby home in the middle of the winter without heat? I was trying not to panic, but I actually did. My other car was sitting in my garage without an engine, we couldn't even afford fixing it. I didn't understand what was going on that year. I decided to call my brother, he was a great mechanic. My brother came over and worked on the car with my husband. They found out that the radiator was clogged and needed cleaning. After few hours the radiator was fixed and the car warmed up in a minute. It happened exactly two days before I went to the hospital.

Galina Cherubin

My little son Eric was born on January twenty ninth, nineteen ninety-seven. He was a healthy eight and a half pound baby. In addition, he was the quietest one out of all my children. He ate well and slept well from the day he was born. I almost didn't lose any sleep at night. Wasn't that a miracle that I got after all those trials during my pregnancy? All the tears and depression that I had didn't affect my baby at all.

Don't you see, my reader, how wonderful God is? He protected this tiny life inside of me while I was getting through all kinds of storms. Many times I look back and see that God has a perfect timing and purpose for everything. He never comes late. I just needed to call upon His name and to have a little bit of faith and He would be right there for me. Never doubt or underestimate God: He will come into your heart the moment you call Him! Amen! Praise be to Him forever and Alleluia!

XXXVII. Back To Low Income

I stayed home with three little children: Alix, 4; Taisa, 2 and newborn Eric. My husband worked hard trying to support us. I noticed that he was loosing weight and even hair. Financial pressure and hard work on the house affected him great deal. I received maternity leave benefits for eight weeks after the birth of Eric. It was half of what I was making when I worked. When I calculated the amount of debts that we had, I was astonished! One thing I knew for sure that I had to come up with payments every month! There was no way that I would let my credit history be ruined! We decided to borrow money from my cousin Lyuda to pay off some of the credit cards. When Eric turned six months old, my cousin asked for her money back. We borrowed the money from her on condition that we will pay back when we can. At that time she told us that she didn't need the money, it was her savings, so we could use it as long as we needed. Everything changed! She gave us a short notice due to her decision of buying a house. Lyuda had no idea of what situation we were in, well, it was her money and she needed it.

I stood in the kitchen when she called… I remember that my arms dropped down powerlessly and I felt that my legs couldn't hold me any more. I sat down on the kitchen floor. "How are we going to do it? I am barely stretching all the ends with my husband's wage. We already took a second mortgage on the house earlier that year. Is that the dead end?" I was so scared; I felt that the depression that I was fighting with all that year was slowly pulling me in again. I didn't know where to go and what to do. What would you do, my dear reader in my situation, just imagine yourself in my place?

After a moment of shock I pulled myself together and remembered how many great things God did for me already. I knew that God was watching over me. I made my strategy clear: I will keep praying and fasting until I receive a response from God. As of that day, I started my intensive daily devotions spending time reading the Bible and praying. I would walk back and forth in my living room with the infant child on my shoulder and talk to God, as He was a person standing right next to me. With the large drops of tears on my eyes I would talk and talk as a desperate child, asking Him for an answer. I knew that He heard me, I also knew that the answer will come at the right time, but my soul was hurting. I guess, I couldn't just admit that the miracle was on the way, I had to see it happen. I knew that I lacked faith, although I believed with my whole being. FAITH is a wonderful spiritual tool given to us by God. The definition of it is "being sure of the things we hope for and knowing that something is real even if we don't see it." I tried to focus on that wonderful Bible promise, but I kind of struggled in receiving these words in my heart. It is so easy to believe in something that we use everyday. When you go to the ATM machine, you believe that it will eject the requested amount of money for you. We always believe that we will get up in the morning and drive to work, or go to the store and purchase groceries. But to believe in a miracle? It's a completely different outlook... Did you ever try to believe in something that cannot be measured by the existing measuring systems? No one invented a periodic table that could calculate the formula of miracles. That's why we call them miracles – unusual, unpredictable, and unexplainable. God is the One who owns the miracle patents, because He invented them. What He asked us to do was – to believe so we could receive His miracles or answers to the prayers. I wished that I had a faith in a size of a mustard seed. If I would, I could tell the mountain to move and it would (Matthew 17:20). I had been asking God for such faith, but so far... I prayed and asked, prayed and asked, day after day, for my miracle to be delivered to my door.

Journey Through Life

I was so ambitious in getting an answer, that I continued my prayers and worship for about two weeks. Every morning I would wake up hoping to see some changes, but everything would be the same as the day before. The same problems, same frustration, same unresolved issues would lie down on my shoulders as a heavy burden. Sometimes I would let the despair to capture my heart when I couldn't see how to pay my cousin back. I continued my prayers with all my efforts.

After two weeks I went to my mailbox and picked up my mail. Among all the bills and the junk mail I found a letter, that I couldn't recognize from the first look. When I opened the envelope, I couldn't believe my own eyes! Was that a trick of one of the sweepstakes promises? No... It looked so real to me! I read it over and over again! It was an offer from the company where I worked. The letter was telling me that I earned some funds that I was never aware of. The sum of the funds equaled to the amount of the money I needed. I couldn't believe my eyes, was that an imagination of a tired mind? It was too good to be true! I couldn't wait for my husband to come back from work to show him the letter. I quickly filled the enclosed form and mailed it back. Two weeks later I received a real check in the sum of the money I needed! It wasn't a mirage or a daydream; it was an answer to my prayers! It was a miracle, delivered straight from heaven to my door. I gave Lyuda her money back and my heart was rejoicing and praising God who fulfilled His promise once again in my life. I cannot even count all the miracles that came to pass in my life. And this one was another confirmation from God that He was watching over my life and He was never late!

The need of second income in my family was growing stronger and one day it became evidently real that I had to go back to work again. I called my mother once again and asked if she could do some more babysitting for me. As usually, she was more than happy to come forward with help AGAIN! God bless my mother! My oldest son Alix was five years old at that time, my daughter Taisa was three and Eric was already nine months old. My mother assured me that she could easily handle my three little youngsters.

The second task was to find a job. I wanted to work for the same company where I worked all these years, therefore I called Human Resources department to see what job openings that had. They promised me to check what was available and to let me know. The recruiter from HR called me one week later and offered a position in a Core Buying department with Genia. When I heard this proposal, I was excited – Genia was one of the people that I would dream to work for! I accepted the offer immediately and one week later I was happily employed. To make my life even easier, my mother moved into my house so I didn't have to drag children back and forth every day. Everything went back to normal; my husband and I worked and we were making enough to cover all our needs at that time. My mother was a generous and trusted babysitter. We finally got a break!

XXXVIII. Masha & Serezha

We were a circle of friends long before we came to the United States. Serezha, nice and quiet Christian young man, was a member of our missionary team. We used to travel a lot together. Serezha got along with everybody. Nobody ever heard him complaining or judging anyone, he was just a happy fellow and everyone respected him. Masha was in our team too. She had a very different personality than Serezha. She was very talkative and loved to laugh a lot. They both were my good friends, although with the very different temperaments. One was as calm as a windless sea, the other was like a high tide.

They came to America at about same time with us and we and remained best friends. We lived in the same city and went to the same church until I met my husband Alix. As good friends, Serezha and Masha both participated in my wedding preparations. The night before my wedding they were helping me with decorating my reception hall.

At that time Serezha's father came from Ukraine to visit his son in the United States and he happened to be one of my wedding guests. From the conversation between Serezha's father and my mother I found out that Serezha wanted to marry me. "Whaaaat?" I couldn't believe my ears! I was really shocked! Sure, we were good friends, but he never revealed his feelings for me. I had no idea what was going through his head during our prolonged friendship. He actually had his eyes on me! Probably, due to his quiet nature, he didn't know how to express his feelings. It was wrong time and place for me to discover Serezha's secrets. My heart already belonged to my husband Alix. I really wished that Serezha found his half among many Christian girls.

Since I got married, Serezha didn't waste any time. Guess what? He started dating Masha right after my wedding!

I was happy for them, I thought that they would be good for each other. About six months later Serezha proposed to Masha and she said that she would love to marry him but she would pray first. She needed to get O.K. from God before she made her final decision. She got a response in a way, "There will be a risk involved in this marriage. You will have a very difficult test in your married life. Would you be able to handle it?" Masha was in love, so she wasn't scared of anything, neither she wanted to change her mind. She told God that she was ready to handle whatever happens in her life. They got married and were a happy family for some time. Serezha was doing roadwork, Masha was raising children.

They had five little children and the youngest one was a little precious girl. She was a spoiled daddy's girl. Every day when Serezha came home from work, she would jump on his lap. Serezha would give her all the attention and love that he had for his little spoiled "sweet pea". He fed her, read her stories and played all kind of games with her. As a wonderful father, he would always find time for all of his children, but the little one had a special place in his heart.

Once after a day of work on the asphalt road under the hot summer sun, he came home very tired but happy as usual. He played with children, ate dinner and then helped his wife to put the little ones to sleep. After the bedtime stories he kissed everybody "Good night" and the house fell into a quiet sleep. At midnight Serezha woke up from a striking pain in his chest.

"Masha, please wake up," he touched the shoulder of his sleeping wife. "Please wake up, something is happening to me. I feel like something burst in my chest. The pain is increasing by a minute."

His desperate voice scared his wife a lot. She heard every word that he said and got off the bed.

Journey Through Life

"Serezha, Serezha, what's wrong?" she almost screamed.

But her husband couldn't say anything else; he fell into a coma. Scared to death, Masha called 911 and the ambulance arrived shortly. Serezha was taken to the nearest hospital. In the hospital he revived and was able to communicate, however, the grasping pain wouldn't go away. The emergency team ran all kinds of tests on him, but they couldn't find anything wrong. After a day in the hospital he was discharged and sent back home. Painkillers reduced his pain, but he continued to suffer a strange discomfort in his chest. Day of confusion and fear passed by and the couple expected that the worst would be over. They didn't know that the following night would bring even more troubles. When the shadows of the night went down Serezha got second pain attack, which was greater than the first one.

"Masha, please call the ambulance, this is serious," he whispered and his head moved down the pillow in another coma.

The ambulance was bringing him to the hospital really fast, but this time they lost his pulse. Doctors couldn't save Serezha this time; he passed away.

Masha heard this shocking news and almost passed out. "Why, why, Jesus, why???" she was saying. "How am I going to handle this tragic loss? What am I going to do with my five little children?" She felt empty, helpless and depressed. Her husband was only forty years old, she didn't expect to lose him that soon. In her grief Masha remembered God's words spoken to her right before she got married. "You will have a very difficult test in your marriage. Would you be able to handle it?" The words were ringing in her ears, "Would you be able to handle it? Would you be able to handle it? Would you be able to handle it?" Masha finally realized that God's prophecy came to pass. She was warned by God, but decided to go for it anyway. Masha prayed and cried a lot, trying to numb her pain. She didn't know where to find strength to go through the tragedy, but she knew that she had to carry this pain for life.

Doctors did an autopsy on Serezha's body. The autopsy showed that he experienced a major stroke. One of the arteries burst in his chest and he died from an internal bleeding.

The children were told that their father would not come back home, because he went to be with Jesus. Children were very sad, how come daddy didn't tell them about it? They were asking Masha if they could visit their daddy sometimes. She told them that one-day they will all meet together in heaven and this will be the greatest and happiest reunion ever. Older children understood their mommy's explanations, but the three-year-old girl insisted that she sees her father and was asking for him every day.

At the burial the little girl saw how the cover was nailed to the casket and the coffin was slowly lowered down into the grave. She pulled herself out of her mother's arms and screamed with her tiny little voice,

"Don't put my daddy in the ground, I love him! Please, let my daddy go!"

A few adults grabbed the little girl and carried her away from the scene. Nobody could quiet her down. Masha had to let her cry until she fell asleep. When she woke up, she remembered that horrible scene of the funeral. She started to scream again,

"Where is my daddy? Why did you let those people put him in the ground? I want my daddy back!"

With the face wet from tears she helplessly looked at her mom. Masha grabbed her little daughter and squeezed her in her arms.

"It's O.K., sweetheart, it's O.K. Your daddy is not in the ground. He escaped and now he is in heaven with Jesus looking down at you from above. You cannot see him but he

Journey Through Life

can see you and even talk to you. One day you will see him again and he will never leave you anymore."

Little girl found that explanation reasonable and stopped crying.

"Is that for real, mommy?" she asked.

"Yes, this is for real, believe me, my little one."

"All right, then I won't cry any more. I just missed sitting on daddy's lap."

She asked her mother for the photo of her daddy and sat for a long time looking at that photo. She kept the photo on her nightstand. Every night before going to bed she had to look at her father's picture and talk to him for a few minutes. Father's smile from the picture would help her fall asleep. She probably dreamed that she was playing with the father and sit on his lap without knowing the fact that her father would not come back.

This story broke Alix's and my heart, I think that it will touch your heart too. Jesus took the place of her father letting her believe that one day they will be together.

I want you, my dear reader, to have the faith of this little girl that one day you will meet all your loved ones in heaven at the great reunion of the church.

XXXIX. An Important Messenger

I had a couple interesting spiritual experiences during my employment with Karton. One of them was my personal meeting with the owner of the company. Of course, I've met the owner many times already. But this was not just saying, "Hi, Mr. Karton," while he was rushing through the hallway with his business portfolio. This story is about a one-on-one meeting with the owner of the company. What was even more important – the motif that brought me to the office of the owner. I simply got an urge to speak with him; I cannot even explain how this idea got into my head? I could not understand why I got these feelings and what I needed to tell him. I was puzzled and decided to pray about it. Day to day my feelings grew stronger but I kept praying.

After a week of prayers I called Mr. K's office and left a message. Mr. K's assistant called me back and scheduled an appointment for me to meet with the owner. I continued praying for God to give me a wisdom and understanding why I needed to meet with this busy and important person? I didn't just want to waste his time… Two days before my appointment I still wasn't sure what I was going to tell him.

"God, help me understand this mission if you are the one sending me there. Why do I need to go there? Was there something special that I had to tell him?"

God sent me an instant answer. He gave me an understanding,

"You are going to minister to the owner about the wonderful things that I did for you."

I spent the night before my appointment in prayer,

"God, thank You for giving me this mission. I want Your name to be glorified in everything I do."

Journey Through Life

In the morning I went to work as usual. In about an hour I looked at the clock, "Oh, I have to go to my meeting, I need to hurry." I had to notify my supervisor and drive to a headquarter building. It was about a mile from the place I worked. When I arrived at Mr. K's office his secretary met me at the door and expressed her apologies.

"Galina," she said. "I am so sorry that you had to drive all the way here. However, Mr. K cannot see you at this moment due to the emergency meeting that just came up. Do you mind coming back in an hour?"

"Sure, no problems," I said. "That's fine with me. I'll be back," and I went back to my working place.

When I returned to Mr. K's office an hour later, he was sitting in his chair and waiting for me. He greeted me in a business manner and asked me to be seated. He apologized for the delay and I noticed a concern in his face. Then I started.

"I am really grateful to work for your company, Mr. K. I know that God brought me here for a purpose."

He was patiently listening to me. His eyes were totally focused on my face. He was probably trying to figure out the purpose of my visit. I gave him my sympathy for his father, who passed away on the day when my daughter was born. I told him that his father was a loving and Godly employer. I told Mr. K about the revelation that I received way before I came to the United States.

"I will never forget these words, "You will be in Karton". At that time I had no idea that Karton existed, but I always kept this mysterious name. When I got employed in Karton, that revelation immediately came up in my mind. I knew that God brought me here and praised Him for His miraculous way of leading me in my life. God knows everything, and our future is in His hands. He is in charge of our past, present and future. Alleluia!"

I kept going on and on with my testimony, and this rich and mighty person was swallowing every word that I said. In silent impression of his face I could read an interest to my story mixed with surprise. That impression stayed on his face for quite awhile. When I finished my speech he finally moved, pushing his chair toward me. "Galina," he said. "Thank you for coming here today and ministering to me because I really needed it. You probably don't know why you are here, but I know that God sent you here to strengthen me. Galina, lets pray together." Mr. K and I held our hands in a short prayer, then he blessed me and I went back to work.

On the following day Mr. K came to my office with an important message for me. He said,

"Galina, right before you came to speak to me yesterday, I had an emergency meeting; remember, I had to delay my meeting with you? A huge problem arose with one of our biggest customers. After your visit and prayer my chief financial officer came to me and announced that the problem was resolved. Thank you, Galina, and may God bless."

When I heard these words from the owner of my company I felt a power going through my body, just as if I was plugged into a power line. A lightning stroked my body top to bottom and I understood that God used me in the right moment to minister to Mr. K. God gave me that urge of speaking to him, that I couldn't ignore. I just had to obey Him and to follow His instructions.

Later that week Mr. K asked me to speak to his Leadership Team.

"I will be more than happy to do that," I replied. "I am always ready to speak about God."

In a week I was scheduled to meet with the Leadership Team of the company. When all Vice Presidents and Executives got together for their routing business meeting they were surprised to find me there waiting for them. I was acquainted with each member of the Leadership Team, but it felt so different when they were together in the red carpeted office to discuss business matters. This time their business meeting was disturbed because I was appointed to do a devotional part of the meeting. I was accompanied by Mark S, Chief Development Officer, who introduced me to the team. Although I knew almost everybody in the room, but I never had a privilege to speak to all of them at the same time. Joe B, Chief Operations Officer, was usually in charge of the LT meetings. This time he was just staring at me trying to understand the purpose of me being there. And he was not the only one. When I looked around, I saw that everybody's eyes were focused on me. They all were trying to figure out the importance that brought me to the meeting. Why did they need to yield the company issues to something that I had to say? And who am I to come and talk to them? All these puzzled looks with evident question marks on their faces? They couldn't wait for a moment to satisfy their curiosity.

After Mark's introduction I didn't take long to start. To break the ice and to release a tension in the room I started with a joke,

"Good Morning. Today I am going to speak in Russian and you try to understand me."

After this phrase everybody broke in laughter.

"Ha-ha-ha! We didn't know that Russians can joke," they pronounced.

Then I continued with my speech, which turned into a serious testimony. I was speaking about all miraculous things that God performed in my father's and my own lives. I felt like the words were coming out of my mouth by themselves. I didn't have to stop and think of what I had to say next – the speech was flowing like a river out of my lips. It was like being connected to a computer; I didn't need to do any thinking but just to let the words out of my mouth. While I was going on with my testimony everybody in the room was very still and quiet. They looked like they were hypnotized by my words. I saw tears on the cheeks of Joe B and a few others. I felt God's presence with me in that room. I knew that God used my mouth to deliver His words to the hearts of all these people in that conference room. I remembered the verse of the Bible that says, "When you brought into the synagogues before the leaders and other powerful people, don't worry about how to defend yourself or what to say. At that time the Holy Spirit will teach you what you must say." Luke 12:11-12. I felt an assurance that this what exactly that was happening to me.

At the end of the speech I threw a challenge to everyone in the room.

"God can use each and everyone in this room for His purpose," I said. "We can move a mountain if we just have faith the size of a mustard seed. Please raise your hands if you don't have faith, because God can fulfill it for you. Amen!" After I said "Amen" nobody moved. They all were in their deepest thoughts. Maybe they were reviewing their lives or maybe they were searching for a source of their faith at that moment? I don't know, I was just a messenger.

Mark S stood up and asked everybody to bow their heads and closed the first part of the meeting in prayer.

I don't know what happened afterwards, it was between them and God, but after that meeting I felt like I grew wings. While driving back to my working place I was flying between the clouds. Beautiful music of praise sounded in my ears and I was singing-along. It was one of the magnificent moments in my life, like I tasted a little piece of heaven. I remembered again that one day when my journey in this world will end, I will be united with Jesus forever and nothing will ever disturb my peace and happiness.

My dear friend if your troubles and tribulations in your life got to an extreme point and you need to taste a piece of heaven – there is an answer to your troubles. And this

Journey Through Life

answer is in Jesus. "I am the Way, and the Truth, and the Life," He said. Everyone who will believe in Him and give his heart to Him will inherit an eternal life. This is not a hard thing to do, just to kneel down and call Him in your prayer. "Anyone who calls on the Lord will be saved." Acts 2:21.

XL.   Pregnant Again!

In February of two thousand I discovered that I was pregnant with my forth child. I always wanted to have a sister for my daughter Taisa since she was asking for a baby sister. I was very excited to have another child and was asking God to let this baby be a little girl. When I went to see my doctor, she asked me if I really wanted to have that baby.

"Yes, of course!" I said. "I have to have another girl!"
She laughed,
"How do you know, Galina, that this will be a girl?"
I responded,
"Just because I ordered a girl."

I was not sure if I convinced my doctor at that time, but I knew that the time will show. A little later at the ultrasound lab I asked the lab assistant for the sex of the baby. She told me, "This is a hundred percent girl!" I was astonished because God answered my prayers once again. The fetus looked healthy and normal and I was about to become a happy mom of four!

There was a little cloud during my pregnancy – one of the tests showed a possibility of Down syndrome in the baby. My doctor referred me to a specialist that would perform Omni-synthesis test to determine if those diagnoses were accurate. The test required a procedure of sticking the needle through the belly and pulling the fluid from the womb. This test would determine if the fetus carried Down syndrome. However, the test had a high risk of either miscarrying the baby or effecting the fetus in other ways. I denied the test. I told my doctor that I would never terminate the pregnancy even if my baby had Down syndrome. I would have the baby no matter what. Besides, I was sure that the baby would be healthy and normal. I also told the doctor that I didn't have a right to abort the life that was created by God, unless God

Journey Through Life

Himself decided to terminate it. I think that this is a huge crime to in front of God to abort lives of innocent unborn children and should be considered as any other kinds of murder.

There were a few other pregnancy-related problems and one of them was my elevated blood sugar. I had to stick to a strict diet and a very strict schedule. I had to have six meals a day and I was not allowed to miss any of them. I measured every cracker and every glass of milk that I had to take. In addition, I had to monitor my blood sugar using "glucometer" two to three times daily. The procedure required sticking the finger with a sharp razor, drawing the blood and measuring it with diabetic strips. It was a really tough procedure. I also had a visiting nurse that came to my house twice a week. No matter how difficult it gets sometimes, there is an end to everything.

Soon my beautiful Christine was born. My first concerns were about her health. "Is she all right?" I asked the doctor. "Does she have Down syndrome?"

I couldn't wait for the doctor to examine Christine and give me a report. When I saw him next time in the door opening I didn't give him a chance to open his mouth first.

"How is she? How is she? Tell me, doctor. Please don't test my patience…" "Please calm down, madam. Your baby is in a perfectly good health."

"Oh, thank God! How about the Down syndrome?"

"Oh, no! Baby does not have the Down syndrome, besides, she has a great reaction, which is a good sign."

Praise God! This was the final piece of evidence that my baby was in a good shape. Great is the Lord! I believed that God would protect my baby girl inside of me – and He did! He reassured me again that those that trust Him would never be forsaken.

After the birth of Christine my blood sugar became normal again. I praised God for that because I needed to put my strength back together to be able to take care of three children plus one newborn. Little-by-little things were getting back in place. My mother-in-law moved into my house and was helping me with my chores. She was bringing my two older children to and back from school. I couldn't go back to work any more. My mother expressed her doubts in babysitting four children for me and I noticed that it was too much for her. She kind of struggled with my three youngsters during my pregnancy. I couldn't ask her for any more help (she was babysitting for me forever, since my first son was born). Therefore, my status changed from working mom to a housewife.

XLI.   September 11

We all grieved after the national tragedy of September eleven. Many of us lost their husbands, wives, children, parents, brothers, sisters or friends. There is no logic explanation to a massive killing by terrorists, except for one – the devil took over their minds and pushed them into this bloody mission. The devil makes slaves out of everyone who follows and worships him. What's really sad is that most of the devil worshipers are not even aware of whom they serve. Those poor and lost souls of terrorists were stolen by the devil, who cheated them and made them human bombs. In addition, the devil made them think that they were doing something good. Tricking people into serving manmade gods, like Allah or any other gods that don't really exist, the devil makes these people foolishly think that they worship their god, but actually they worship the devil. He takes the place of their lifeless gods and makes them do all horrible and ugly things.

Real God, the Creator of the world never asks anyone to hurt or offend anybody, because our God is LOVE and this will never change. No matter how far human beings walk away from God, He will always love them. He loves those who curse Him, those who betray Him, those who pierced the ugly nails through His body on the cross. God never hates anybody, because He is the source of LOVE.

Too bad we don't live in heaven where none-of the evil things exist. We live in this world, where GOOD fights with EVIL all the time. In many cases EVIL wins, because a lot of people denied God and denied GOOD.

On September eleven early in the morning my husband went to work. His shift used to start really early, between four and six a.m. That day he was scheduled to deliver something to New York City. Waiting in the office for his truck to get loaded he said a prayer. He asked God to bless his new day, especially because he had to make a trip out of state. After some waiting Alix's supervisor told him that the trip was cancelled. Instead of routing deliveries company authorities arranged a training day for all drivers. My husband didn't mind training, since he was a new employee. "Training is training, doesn't matter if the trip was cancelled..." He settled himself to listen to the instructor for a few hours.

After an hour of training, everyone was requested to move from the training area to the Media center. All TV's were turned on and reporters were announcing the sad news – the New York towers were hit by a terrorist plane. When my husband heard this news his heart stopped beating. He closed his eyes and said a prayer about all the victims of the terrorist war. He also thanked God for canceling his trip to New York. He understood that God protected him from all the problems and confusions that were happening in New York City that day.

After that horrible day, my brother-in-law Anatoly met with one Indian Christian lady Gracy who told him a testimony about how God wonderfully protected her, as He protects everybody that trusted Him. Gracy graduated from a college and was looking for a job. She applied in many different places and employers were calling her for interviews. It was year two thousand, the end of the millennium, and many employers were looking for graduates with computer major. Gracy was invited for an interview in the World Trade Center. The interviewer favored Gracy's education and skills and she was offered a job there. She was very happy and excited about this offer and very anxious to start her new job. But before accepting the offer she decided to pray about it. God said, "No. Don't take this job, otherwise, you will be in great trouble."

This wasn't the answer that she was looking for; she was disappointed. She argued with God, saying that she really wanted to work in the World Trade Center. She didn't know

Journey Through Life

if she could find anything better than this offer. But she refused the offer because she trusted God.

Gracy took a job, which was her second option and went on with her life. On September eleven, a year after her application, she heard the shocking news. A place where she dreamed to work was cruelly destroyed by terrorists. Then she realized how God saved her from the horrible tragedy and cried for hours. She told my brother-in-law that she didn't know how to thank God for this miraculous deliverance.

The New York towers, the symbol of pride and strength of the nation, were destroyed in an hour by the terrorist act. Who would ever think that the World Trade Center would turn into a pile of dirt and debris? The treasures of American people disappeared in a very short moment, leaving terror and death behind. How many lives ended at that bloody pile! People just like us couldn't even imagine that morning that they would never see another day. God observes the future and sees the danger in our paths. He reveals it to His servants, who pray and look for answers. The prophecy of David Wilkerson came to pass, "New York City will be in fire." New York City never before saw that kind of fire and destruction that happened on September eleven. It wasn't just a fire, it was a war.

My dear reader, if you care about your life, turn it to Jesus. Nobody else in the Universe could guarantee protection in this world and even more, which is eternal life, like Jesus does. Amen!

XLII. Down The Hill Once Again

From the time I stopped working, our financial situation got worse. We had no choice but to sell our house. We met with a Real Estate agent and signed a selling agreement. Christine turned nine-month old; she was a beautiful addition to our family. My older daughter Taisa was very glad about having a sister. She was doing everything to help me with the baby. I said to myself, "Now I have a complete family: two boys and two girls – everybody has somebody to play with." My husband and I enjoyed the children and everything would be fine if we had a little more money to pay our bills. But the money issue was a fast growing issue. We struggled even more from the moment when my maternity benefits stopped. The only hope was the house, if it sells, we would pay off all our debts. But things don't always happen the way we want them to happen. God was testing our patience and I knew that. I also knew that He was never late. Sometimes I tried to ask God to speed up the process, but He always had perfect timing for everything. The problem with us, people, is that we usually don't have enough patience to wait for God's terms. Too bad! You cannot bypass God. There is nothing you can do if He decides that the time is not right yet. I learned from my own mistakes and experiences that the best thing is to trust God in everything.

Many people came and looked at the house from multiple real estates, but they would go back the same way they came. The visitations were increasing and I found myself scrubbing, straightening out the house and preparing it for showing all the time. Considering that I had to drive my two older ones to/from school three times daily plus to take care of two little ones, I barely managed my regular schedule with the schedule of Real Estate visitations. It was such a busy time period that I was getting exhausted physically and emotionally. Physically – due to all the work that I had to do, emotionally – because of our financial shortages and the growing credit card debts.

My husband worked very hard to make a living for us, but we finally realized that his salary wasn't enough to cover our expenses. Alix and I decided that he had to look for another job. After about a month of searching through all the employment articles and Internet pages my husband finally found a job that paid much more than the one he had. He made the decision of quitting his job and starting the new one as soon as he could. He was hired there as a commercial driver. The first few weeks we were all excited of him making about hundred-dollars more a week than at his previous job. It was not quite what we actually needed for our family, but it was much better than before. We tried to squeeze our needs into a smaller budget and thought that this would be all right at least until we sell the house. Our calculations worked out for some time, but then my husband was placed on some kind of flex program. His supervisor told him that they are switching him to a position called "on-call" driver, which meant that he didn't have a permanent schedule. Alix didn't like it that much but had no choice. His supervisor would call him to work any morning or afternoon as needed. Very soon we figured out that the "on-call" hours reduced to three or four hours a day. "Oh, Lord!" I said. "This was supposed to be a full time job! What is happening? What are we going to do now?" His job became part-time work. Our financial situation got more severe; we had no choice but to borrow more money from credit cards to pay our bills. Alix was not wasting his time; he started to look for a new job. After two months he quit and moved to V- Company. However, V-Company required every new employee to be trained for eight weeks prior to letting them work on their own. For the training time they paid between forty and sixty dollars a day.

Alix was determined to get through the training time and see what to expect next. The job requirements were to transport powder materials from point A to point B. The starting hours were as early as four a.m. Since he needed two hours to drive to his work, he had to be up at one a.m. to get there on time. He would finish his job at four or five p.m. and by the time he would get home, it would be six-seven p.m. There was no time for anything but work; not even enough time for sleep. When Alix got his first paycheck, it was only two hundred dollars. Wow! Was this a joke? We were hoping that after eight weeks this would change. When he heard that after the training period he wouldn't be paid per hour but per load, he lost his hope again. Alix purchased a newspaper and started to look for another job once again. After a few weeks he quit V-Company and started a new career in P- transportation services. He started there as a commercial driver. "Finally! I finally made it!" he said to himself. We were all happy and excited about this successful move. Slowly recovering from the financial crisis, we were getting back on our feet and praised God for his help. Alix's salary increased, it was almost equal to our join salaries when we both worked. We caught up with the monthly payments without borrowing from credit cards. Although, our total debts were outrageous, we could still deal with our monthly minimums. Two months passed of Alix's career in P- transportation services. We were approaching December of two thousand and two. Alix was at the end of his ninety-day trial period. I couldn't wait for him to receive the benefit package, which supposed to include health insurance coverage for the family. We were making plans on how to fight the debts. We also hoped that we could even get the Christmas gifts for the children. We had enough troubles that year, could that be a break for us? We were desperate to get to the end of our trials, like anyone would be in this situation. Of course, nobody knows the future, only God does; and many times He put us through

Journey Through Life

trials to test our faith. Trials are part of Christian life and they are mandatory. But trials build up the character and the faith. Its like the burned gold gets purified, Christians become stronger after the trials.

One December morning, I was feeding my little one and looking in the window where I could see the full view of the driveway. Suddenly I saw my husband's car backing up on the driveway.

"It's interesting," I said. "It's only eleven a.m. What is he doing home at this time? Maybe he got a day off to buy Christmas presents for children?"

I was guessing...

"Honey, what are you doing home at this time?" I asked when he walked in the front door.

"Is everything all right?"

"Not really," Alix responded with the note of despair in his voice. "I got fired." Shockingly looking at him I was trying to see if he was joking (he used to do that a lot!). Too bad, it wasn't a joke! It was a hard and burning truth! I held on to the chair.

"How could they?" I almost screamed. "Two weeks before Christmas you are thrown out of your job? I thought you were one of the best drivers?"

I remembered that Alix was getting compliments from everybody at his job. Even drivers told him, "Well, they like you here. You do an excellent job!" Alix was almost sure that due to his performance and his ability to go along with everybody nothing could happen to him. He really thought that he would hold on to this job, even though, it required working sixty hours a week.

That day he went to work in his usual good spirit, besides, it was Friday. While waiting for the truck to be loaded, he was looking for a hand jack which was a "must" tool in delivering the product inside elevators. He found a hand jack and locked it to a pole with his little lock while taking care of the paperwork. When he got back to his jack, it wasn't there any more, besides, someone took his lock. He went to his supervisor to see if he knew what happened to the jack. Before Alix opened his mouth, the supervisor lifted his head and started yelling,

"Don't you ever lock my jack!"

Alix was trying to say that he needed a jack for his deliveries, but supervisor didn't want to hear anything. It was humiliating for him to listen to the excuses of one simple guy. My husband said,

"Sorry, but at least give me my lock back, please."

At that point the supervisor exploded all the anger on Alix's head.

"I see that you don't get it! You don't want to work! You just came here to argue with me! Nobody can argue with me, because I am in charge of this place! Go home and I never want to see you again or I will call the security!"

"Are you firing me?" Alix asked.

"Yes, I am! You are fired! Go home!"

He turned around and walked away, not giving even one little thought to the action that he just did. He didn't care if he caused any pain to the person.

Humanity cannot get rid of the evil roots, because the devil is still functioning in his full power on Earth. The only way of beating the evil is to bring Christ in our lives, because nobody can beat the POWER OF CHRIST!

The bad news hit me like a thunder from the bright and sunny sky. I felt that it was the last drop in the cup of patience and my faith was melting down like a piece of ice on the sun. This is it! Two weeks before Christmas we lost our last income, our last hope and last strength. My husband didn't want to show me his fear – he needed to be strong for all of us. (Later he confessed to me that he was confused himself and also scared of not knowing what to do next.)

Journey Through Life

"My children will not get Christmas gifts this year," I whispered and my heart fell somewhere deeply down. But what was even worse – we were one foot away from loosing our house. We had no savings and credit cards were full to the limits. I felt like we were standing at the end of the cliff, therefore, I just fell on my knees as a hopeless child and whispered a prayer. My husband joined me and we prayed together until we ran out of words. Then I remembered words from the Bible, "Even if I walk through a very dark valley, I will not be afraid, because You are with me. Your rod and your walking stick comfort me." Psalm 23:4. At times like this, when all possibilities are exhausted, there is no other choice but to trust God. And I started to build a vision on how could we escape the troubles, actually, I was building a road to faith. When we finished the prayer, we went to bed with hope that the following day would bring better news for us.

As I said earlier, our house was on the market for almost a year – people were coming and going – that's about it. We got a few offers, but they were not good enough for us to repay our debts. We didn't even hope to make any money on the house, we were just trying to come out of debts.

On the next day after my husband's ended carrier, I woke up brokenhearted. It was the same usual bright and sunny morning, but nothing was the same for me. All these clouds of worries and fears were pressing my shoulders down as a heavy burden. I didn't know how to get through the day and where to get strength to take care of children. Trying not to think about yesterday's events, I got out of the room. Alix too was avoiding talking to me about yesterday. He and I knelt down in prayer, giving all our troubles to Jesus.

Later that morning my realtor called and asked if I could meet with some other people that wanted to see my house. I didn't care about visitors that much – so many of them came and left, I gained nothing except extra cleaning work over and over again. In addition, I didn't have any strength to clean the house that day. But in spite of everything, I said, "Well, all right. They could come."

A few hours later a husband and wife, accompanied by my realtor, knocked on the door. They looked at the house in details, asked a lot of questions. Then they walked through the house for the second time. After all, they came out through the patio door and spent almost half an hour in the back yard. They seemed to be interested but I didn't want to put my hopes too high. The same evening my realtor called me and announced the news – the couple gave full offer on the house. I couldn't believe my ears, but it was true. "The only thing is," he said, "we just need to wait for a few days until everything is documented and then it will become official." It was overwhelming! All right! I knew that God had an answer for us! The day after my husband lost his job God sent a buyer for our house! One more prophecy came to pass! It was just months ago when I spoke with one of my friends and asked her to pray for our house that was on the market for so long. Then she got back to me with theWord from God, saying, "This burden is a huge stone that you cannot move physically. Besides, you cannot go around it or go over it, because it's so huge! Pray and God will remove this stone from your way." That December day God was about to remove that stone! This is not a fiction or a made up story, this is a true story from my own experience, my reader. And I want you to hear me; "God never comes late to those that love Him."

My husband decided to apply for unemployment benefits, since he had no fault in loosing his job. When UC department requested employer to give them a reason of Alix's termination, they replied that Alix was fired due to his poor performance. It was such a lie! These evil people fired my husband without any reason, and now they were trying to justify their actions in front of the authorities. When it

Journey Through Life

comes to children of God, evil never wins! The employer could never prove my husband's poor performance, because there was no proof! After a little struggle my husband was qualified to receive twenty-six weeks of unemployment compensation. God is great!

When evil people don't succeed in something, it makes them mad and angry. The last attempt of the employer to get back at my husband was withholding Alix's last paycheck. I had to get involved and called all the offices of the company, but the only person that was ever available was just a switchboard operator. Mister K., the director of Human Resources, never answered his phone and never returned our calls. After a week of attempts to communicate with someone in the company, I just got tired. There was no one ever available, it was a complete gridlock! When I called Payroll there was only answering machine. Then I came up with an idea. I decided to call Payroll every five minutes for about two hours. "If nobody answers, I would just leave a message every time I call," I said to myself. "When they get tired of listening to my messages, they would have to call back." So I did! I called them every five minutes and recorded multiple messages. In my messages I warned them that I would report them to the Department of Labor if they didn't reply. I thought that I used the entire recording tape. An hour later Payroll representative called me back and assured me that he would take care of Alix's paycheck. That was the last breakthrough with P- Transportation Company and we never had to deal with them again. I hope my dear reader that you never have to meet with this kind of people, like Alix did.

XLIII. Busy Winter

Alix became unemployed and it was a great timing for him to stay home. Our house had to be prepared for inspection and sale and this was a full time job for my husband and me. We were given six weeks to move out of the house. I was packing like crazy! I never knew that I had so much stuff until I had to move. Boxes one after the other were packed and transported to my mother's garage – praise God for that free storage. Every day on my way to school I would bring five/six boxes to my mother. My husband didn't have time to do any of the packing, he made himself busy with repairs. He had to bring the house to a level of perfection. He found all kind of little jobs in the house that even I had to assist him with delivering materials from The Home Depot. I didn't know any more who I was: full time mom of four little ones, express carrier, deliverer of home improvement materials, packer and so on… I just knew that every day I was in competition with time. Praise God that He gave me strong feet and good health. I used my efficiency to the maximum to make everything work.

The settlement day was around the corner, but we still had a mount of packing and cleaning to do. My husband ordered a Dumpster that was supposed to take all the junk from the garage and the shed. We also dumped there our old furniture. In order to fit everything in the Dumpster, we had to break every piece of furniture. I remember holding a hammer in my hands and crushing old chests, book shelves and other things that needed to be taken apart. My children had a lot of fun helping us with the furniture breaking business. Soon the container was filled up to the top – it was just the right size. We were very tired but had no chance to rest – we had to accomplish much more. In the evening I barely got to my bed… What am I talking about? Our beds were gone! What we had left were a few heavy blankets

Journey Through Life

that served us as beds for the last three nights. It was all right to sleep on the floor with uplifted spirit. Although our bodies were exhausted from that move, but emotionally we were very excited. I couldn't wait to see myself signing the settlement documents.

The settlement day approached and we were almost flying behind the steering wheel of our car to the place of settlement. I remember that critical hour of exchanging documents from seller to buyer. I remember that lightness that I felt after that heavy mortgage load fell off my shoulders. I felt free again! Debt free! Actually, with the money that we got back we paid off our mortgage and most of our credit cards. I was not scared of my future, because I learned to trust God in taking control over my life. After that crucial year when problems were hitting me one after the other and I didn't know how to win that war, God comforted me again, "Don't worry, I will remove this stone from your way, because I love you. The only thing you need to do is pray and trust in Me." From the moment God talked to me I prayed and prayed and prayed… until the settlement day, when God removed the stone from my way and I came out as free as a bird. One more prophecy came to pass in my life. Thank You, Jesus, again and again for Your supernatural power that makes miracles happen in our lives.

We moved to Alix's cousin's house where we occupied two rooms on the third floor. This was our temporary residence until we came up with the decision what to do next. Roosevelt, Alix's cousin, was in about same age as Alix. Since Alix didn't have a brother to play with, he grew up with Roosevelt, considering him a brother. The brotherhood of two cousins never changed, although they were all grown up. They lived close to each other and deal with each other well. Roosevelt was living in a huge colonial house in the suburb of Philadelphia. Being just a single owner of a big house, he offered us a place to stay. It was really nice of him to accommodate our big family for awhile.

We finally settled in Roosevelt's house and my husband and I took a wonderful time of rest. We needed it very much after all that hard work! We thanked God for His deliverance and also thanked Roosevelt for his gracious response to our need.

Soon after, we started to think what to do next. Meanwhile, Alix's aunt bought a house in Orlando, Florida. One day she called us and asked to come and visit her. Then she called again and again. Finally, she offered us to move in with her.

"Wow!" I said. "Is that the sign for us to move to Florida?"

We decided to pray and seek God's directions. "God, is this the way that You want us to go? Please reveal us what You have for us in the future. Thank you, dear Jesus." After two weeks we received a letter from my homeland. The letter had a revelation for us. "You asked Me to help you with the decision that you have to make. Yes, you need to move to the place that you are thinking about. You will still have some difficulties, but I will be with you everywhere. I will shed my light everywhere you go." Now we knew that our destination was Florida and thanked God for revealing that to us. We decided to wait until children's school season was finished and then we would go.

In March of two thousand and two during the spring break we went to Orlando, Florida and spent some quality family time in Alix aunt's house. We also enjoyed the places that we visited in the southern part of Florida at that beautiful time of the year. My children were very excited to go to MGM studios for the first time. Then we went to Gatorland where we had a lot of fun watching all kind of shows with alligators. My mother and my sister Irena accompanied us in our trip. My mother had Russian friends

Journey Through Life

that lived on the Mexican Gulf side of Florida. Since it was close by, she insisted that we visit her friends. We all agreed and soon we were on the way to North Port, Sarasota County. It was a good experience for us to learn some more about Florida. When we took River Road exit toward North Port, we were amazed of how spacious was the land and how nice was the nature in this part of the state. All of the surroundings attracted our eyes so much that we couldn't stop enjoying it. River Road runs through fields, parks and natural reserves. You cold see a beautiful touch of God's hands everywhere. How beautifully was everything created for us to enjoy this precious God's gift! "Where is the city?" I asked. It felt like we were traveling through "no man's land". Soon we started to see some buildings and houses. Oh, that's where the city of North Port was! It was hiding from us behind the trees! The city was the size of a small town. However, it had everything in it, just like in a regular city. When we drove through North Port, we noticed a lot of developments everywhere, but there was still a large area of undeveloped lands. The populated areas were mixed with natural parks and farmlands. Parks, rivers, lakes and canals were everywhere in the city. It looked so unique and so precious that we fell in love with this beautiful landscape as soon as we saw it. A few miles away were Gulf beaches with unusually clear water. New houses were built everywhere throughout the city. I was told that North Port was the fastest growing city in Florida. Due to migration from the Northern States, the population majority were not born Floridians. My husband told me, "I feel like this place is for us. I feel that we will be moving here." "I wish," I responded, since I really liked the town.

After that trip was over we continued to pray to God asking Him for more detailed directions. It was two months prior to the end of the school season and we really needed to start making arrangements for our interstate move. Alix's aunt offered to sell her house to us, but Alix wasn't sure if we should buy a house right away. Alix and I thought that we had to find the rent first until we settle with jobs, school, etc.

"How could we buy a house without knowing if you can find a job?" I asked my husband.

"That's true," he said. "We have to settle first."

We didn't give Alix's aunt straight answer. She saw our hesitation and sold the house to someone else.

With everything going on I started to get confused. I was trying to figure out what is that God wanted us to do. When God told us that Florida was our destination we put our hopes on renting some space in Alix's aunt house. However, that deal didn't work out, that house was sold. What do we do and where do we go? I was searching for more answers from God… Finally, Alix came up with an idea. "Why don't you call your mother's friends," he told me, "and ask them to look for an apartment for us in North Port? If this is God's plan, everything will work. Otherwise, we have to do something else."

I agreed, "All right, I will start calling." I called one of my family childhood friends Anatoly and asked him for a favor. "I don't care if it's as small as two bedroom," I said. "We just need a place to land."

He promised me to look around and to let me know what was available. Meanwhile, we were praying and hoping to hear good news from North Port. We needed an affordable place that would not be higher than five hundred and fifty dollars a month.

Anatoly asked his brother-in-law Yury to help him look, since Yury already deal with the Real Estate office. Yury found a couple apartments for us, however, they didn't fit our needs. The first apartment was not available until August, but our deadline was mid-June. The second apartment required the tenants to be employed in Florida.

Journey Through Life

"God," I asked. "This couldn't be a conflict! Didn't You tell us that Florida was our destination?"

But God was just testing our patience. Yury never gave up on helping us.

"Well," he said. "Let's try option "C".

He decided to go to the Russian community and ask if they had any apartments for rent. He found out that there was an apartment that could be available by the end of May. The tenants were not sure yet if they would be moving out by that time. Anyway, they promised us to give their final answer by May twentieth. Alix and I hesitated.

"Does it worth to wait for two weeks just for an answer? What if the answer is negative?"

But then Yury told me that the rent would cost us five hundred and fifty dollars, including utilities. Whaaaaat? That what we asked for! It couldn't be true! We decided to wait. On May twentieth I called Yury and got a positive response. Apartment will be available for us by June first! When we got in touch with the landlord, he told us that he would charge us five hundred and fifteen dollars instead. "Thank You, Jesus! You heard us and answered again in a wonderful way! We even got it for less than we asked for!"

We were absolutely convinced that the move to Florida was the right move. On June fourteenth we loaded the Rider truck and started our travels. My youngest twenty-months-old daughter was traveling with us. The other three children were staying over my brother's house in New Jersey. When we completed our move we went back to pick up the rest of the family. My second youngest five-year-old son Eric was so happy to see us that he would not walk away from our van. He wanted to make sure that we wouldn't leave him again. Finally, we were all together on the way to our new home in Florida!

Right before our final move I received a letter from Pennsylvania UC department. The letter was notifying me that I was eligible to receive thirteen months of extended UC benefits, according to the document signed by George Bush. It was God's gift for us. We listened to His words and followed His directions and He actually supported us and provided for our needs. Alix was receiving his regular unemployment benefits and I started to receive thirteen weeks of the extended ones. We were receiving two incomes at the time when our lives were making a sharp turn. When our benefits got exhausted, at the end of June, we found out that Alix was eligible for his three months extension. Furthermore, I happened to receive Tier II extension for another three months. Praise God! We were covered all the way until the end of September! God knew that we needed time to settle in a new place and He took care of this ahead of time. It was a financial miracle for us at the right time.

XLIV.   Coming To Florida

Settling in the new state brought us some disappointments. Our rental house was not up to date. It was built about thirty years ago and needed some maintenance. As soon as I turned the faucet handle in the bathroom, I figured out that there was no water in the house. What happened to the water? I called our next door neighbors that occupied the other side of this twin house and asked if they had the same problem. They told us that four days ago there was an explosion somewhere in the utility room that was caused by a strong lightning. Since then the water disappeared. Our neighbors called the landlord, who lived in Canada, and told him about the problem. As a retired plumber, the owner decided to take care of this problem himself. It took him about a week to get to Florida by bus (bus was his preferred type of transportation).

We were figuring out what to do without water in the house. We prayed that God wouldn't let our enemy break our faith. We didn't want any discouragement to ruin our happiness and excitement.

On first day we had to buy water for cooking and saved some rainwater for other needs. On the following day our neighbors went out to hunt for the water around the neighborhood and they succeeded. A hose was pulled between two properties and we got running water in the house. After a week the owner arrived and fixed the problem. People may call it "luck", but the Christians call it "blessing from God" or "answer to prayers". It was an answer, because we asked.

Since our landlord Gregory lived in Canada, our neighbors introduced us to him right after he arrived. He was a little man in his late eighties with a very pleasant smile. In spite of his age, he was a very active and energetic person. From the first day of his arrival he started to take care of the household. In a short time he repaired a lot of things in the house, including the pipe that burst from the lightning strike. He replaced old sinks and vanities for us so we would feel comfortable. He even ordered a new storage shed for us when he saw how much stuff we brought with us. God opened this man's heart and gave him a desire to do those improvements for us. He also gave us an additional room on the back of the house and he let us use that space to store our remaining luggage. After a month of settling down, we found ourselves very comfortable in this inexpensive rental home.

September was our month of revival and thanks to God for all the blessings that we received that year. It was a month of reading the Word, fasting and praying. We took time to thank God for all the answered prayers and asked Him to be with us in our future. Here we were new residents of a small Florida town, waiting for the next miracle from God. He had never forsaken us and will never leave us in the future.

If you, my dear reader, would like to experience miracles in your life, you don't need to go far – God is omnipresent. He is looking for those who are willing to open their hearts and let Him in. He will come in and will be your guide and sponsor and will lead you in the right direction of your life. When you experience God's love and power, you will never regret searching for Him.

<u>XLV.   He Is Never Late!</u>

While we were receiving unemployment benefits, we had to make some major decisions on what to do for a living. Look for a job? Buy a land and build a house or purchase an existing house? What was our main purpose of coming all the way here? We had to prioritize our problems and figure out what to do next.

We drove around the city many times, studying areas and neighborhoods. We loved the city and were looking if we could purchase a vacant land. There was one three-acre lot for sale. It was located in a wooden area next to the city Estates. It was a very nice and private area, so we decided to get information about that particular lot. The realtor told us that this was the only available lot in acreage in that area at that time. The price of the lot was thirty-six thousand dollars. We were also told that someone was already asking for it. We got so anxious about purchasing that lot that we forgot about our other priorities. I scheduled an appointment with the Real Estate agent for Saturday morning. I was told to come there early before the other party arrived. We prayed before my appointment and I went to meet with the agent. I filled out Buyer Agreement; however, bank was closed on Saturday so I couldn't bring a required downpayment with me. I promised to do that first thing Monday morning. The lady realtor was very nice to me. She told me not to worry, but to come back on Monday with the downpayment.

The whole day on Sunday we prayed about this deal. We asked God to bless this purchase if it was His will, otherwise, to stop us from getting it. We didn't want to go into something that we wouldn't be able to handle. I ran to the bank on Monday morning. That's when I learned that the bank's system was down. I was told that for some reason all banks in this branch along the East Coast experienced the same problem. No transactions could be done at that time.

I was told to come back an hour later. I was so anxious to complete that transaction that I couldn't wait for the bank system to be fixed. I called the realtor and told her that I will be in as soon as I process my bank transaction. In the afternoon the bank was functioning again. Prior to making a withdraw I called the realtor again, notifying that I was coming with my check deposit. There was a slight silence on the other side of the line. I didn't know that the realtor was preparing a huge disappointment for me. She told me that due to the delay with my deposit, she couldn't hold the property and someone else already purchased it. I was not pleased to hear that after all the efforts that I had to put into it!

When I thought more about it, I realized that God didn't let us purchase that lot. He simply stopped us by shutting the bank systems down. It was, probably, wrong timing for us to buy a property, since we didn't have an established income yet. We understood that this was a very clear answer to our prayer. It's always good to council with all-powerful God. He will always protect us from making mistakes.

Alix and I decided to stop hunting after buildings and properties and wait for the right time. We counted on God's grace and mercy and we knew that He would show us the purpose of coming all the way here. I believed that we were on our way to that purpose.

At one point of my life when we sold our house in Pennsylvania, I thought that we were through with the financial straggles. I never expected to get in the same hole again. It was my determination not to slide down into excessive debts again, not under any conditions! I was holding on to this principal as hard as I could. My husband and I did everything possible to pay off our remaining credit card balances. We succeeded with that task for a while and managed to pay off some of our "tails", but then ... everything changed.

Journey Through Life

From the time that we sold our house we owed somewhat decent sum of money to the credit card – about six thousand dollars. This debt wasn't as significant as the one we had before, therefore, I was more than sure that we could conquer it. I was hoping that we would beat it very soon, however, it didn't happen as I expected. We had some savings that we could use to repay that balance but we couldn't touch our funds until we settle in the new state. Making a living in another state was just like starting all over again. The only source that we could live on was our savings account.

My husband was without job, by that time our savings were gone. Instead of paying our debts, we were adding more to them. It was discouraging to see how our debts were accumulating again. I suffered a lot from the financial burdens; I didn't want to carry the same type of burden again. I started to sell stuff from my garage and storage... Those attempts gave us kind of relief, but it was just the temporary one. There was nothing more that I could do about changing the situation, besides the things that I had already done. After a while I ran out of ideas of what else I could possibly do to rescue our finances... I went on my knees again...

I continued praying intensively. I wanted to understand God's language, but many times I would get so confused. Many times I got to the point of not knowing what to do and I would feel a bitter lump in my throat again. Some days my brain was blank, just like a blank sheet of paper. I was desperate again to hear from God. I remember kneeling down, but the words stuck in my mouth and I didn't know what to say. I stood on my knees silently for quite awhile. My mind was floating somewhere without any directions. I was looking for a sense of my existence. And then I felt like the roaring waters cut the way through my brain and gushed out of my eyes. I don't remember how long I cried, but suddenly I gained my speech back. "Oh, God, please hear me like You did before. Our benefits are running out, and we are facing a dead end again. What do you want us to do next? God, please don't let us face a financial crisis. Please talk to me...I need to support my family, and be a blessing to others. I would like to support ministries, people in need, etc. God, please give me an answer, give it to me in any way You want to: through dream, through a preacher or through Your Word. Please, God... Thank You. Amen."

My face was washed out but I felt an ease in my heart. I knew that God's answer was near. I knew that coming to Florida was not a mistake, but His will, because He sent us here. And I was trying to practice my faith.

After the prayer I picked up my little box of Bible verses "Daily Bread." I put my hand on the box, said a short prayer, and pulled out the verse. The verse was Second Corinthians 9:8, "And God can give you more blessings than you need. Then you will always have plenty of everything – enough to give to every good work." Warm faith filled my heart – from that moment I knew that help was on the way, it was just the matter of time. God answered my prayer instantly with His powerful Word! I just had to be patient and wait. Sometimes we don't realize how powerful and great God is and how close He is to our needs.

God heard my prayers and came forward with an answer. My husband was offered a job in a major company and this was already a relief. I got a part-time job (I couldn't do full time with my four little kids). This was another relief.

We occupied half of two-bedroom twin house and it was very tight for the family of six. At the beginning we could manage it, but then we started to have a feel that it was too packed for us. Plus we wanted to stop paying rent, which we did for about eighteen months, we had to get a house on our own. We started searching for an affordable house. I wouldn't say that we couldn't find such a house, but for some reason we couldn't get one. Every time when we found a decent house we would find out that it was taken by somebody else from "under our nose". We got disappointed time after time when realtor told us over and over again that the house that we wanted had an offer already. We missed maybe seven houses for just because we happened to be late, about a day or two... These disappointments made a crack in the foundation of my hope, which gave a leak to a fear again. "What if we cannot afford to buy a house anymore? The prices are going up like crazy! What do we do next?" Every time I tried to encourage myself with the words that God was taking care of us, but the other voice, the voice of fear would whisper in my ears, "Look around, this is the reality, you have no hope..." I went through battle after battle, it was just like a war. But I never stopped trusting God and He came forward.

During all this warfare I shared my concerns with my Pastor and he said,

"Galina, there is a house that a lady from our church is selling. Why don't you look at it."

"Oh, really? Thank you for telling me, I will check it out," I said.

My husband and I went to see that house and... we both decided that it was everything we needed and everything we could afford. We gave an offer right away and started to process paperwork. It wasn't as easy as we thought, but we could see the light at the end of the tunnel.

Meanwhile, we started to pack our belongings. After signing the purchase contract we found out that the house that we rented was sold. Believe me or not, but it was sold overnight. A family came from the one of the northern states and purchased that house. It was quite a shock for us, but there was more... New owners approached us and requested that we move out in two weeks. Two weeks? I couldn't do it with my four little children even if I wanted to. I was devastated! "Are you serious?" I proclaimed defensively.

"The minimum time you should give us is one month." It was a struggle to convince them, but at the same time we were glad that our settlement day was coming in four weeks. It wasn't a smooth process for us at all, but I don't think I ever got anything easy in my life. Therefore my body developed strong "anti-biotics" to all kinds of hardships. The main thing was that I always had a happy ending, just like in a fairytale.

XLVI. Happy Ending

I was very excited and thankful to God for another victory that He let us to experience in our lives. How sweet was the feeling of moving into our own house after two years of unsettled and uncomfortable life. Living on rent was like sitting in the airport and waiting for the next flight. If you happen to see the movie, "The Terminal", it shows all the hardships that Tom Hanks' character Peter experienced during his prolonged waiting time in the terminal. That was the similar kind of life as we were living in our rental house. The hardest thing about being tenants was that we couldn't change or improve anything that was happening around us. We completely depended on the landlord, who was away six months out of twelve. Not able to improve living conditions of that place or to prevent systems from breaking down on us, we just had to endure and be patient. I am a very independent individual, although I am very social too. It bothered me a great deal when things didn't go right and I had "no say" about it.

It was a huge relief for us to have our own place under the sun, where my husband and I were in charge. We finally got a privilege to manage our house on our own. For about a month we were flying on the wings of our fulfilled hopes... until the time of our first mortgage payment. It's difficult when the cruel reality cuts in your perfect peace and cuts off the happiness that you received after long time of trials. Enemy never wants us to stay happy and excited for a long time. At this point the adversary cut out a large piece of a perfectly baked cake.

The time came for me to sit down and review my budget. What I was the most afraid of happened. Our expenses exceeded our income! What could we do? Borrow again? Oh, no! God, please don't put us through the same trials that we suffered for years! There has to be a way out of this swamp...

Our powerful God knew the depth of our long suffering and heard our desperate voices... It didn't take long for us to receive an answer from Him this time. Miraculously we paid off all of our outstanding debts and finally we were DEBT FREE! Praise the Lord for everything He had done for us. If it weren't for Him, I would probably hit the bottom of this life.

When I observe the human life in a global perspective, I see it as a journey given to us by God. This line segment of time called "LIFE" does not end with death. This line continues indefinitely, although many people mistakenly think that death is the end. No, it is not the end. Believe me, my dear friend, death is just the beginning of an eternal life. It is up to you to choose between the happy ending or the horrible one. Everyone who accepts Christ as his personal Savior will always get a happy ending – eternal paradise with Christ. However, if you walk away from Christ, you walk away from the treasures that heaven could offer. There is a horrible place called hell, and it will swallow you no matter if you believe it or not. I am not trying to tell you any monstrous stories, but the truth! While you are still alive you still have time to make your choice – HEAVEN or HELL!

Alix and I opened the Bible and read the story of Moses again. God performed many miracles for Israelites before He took this nation out of Egypt. God opened the Red Sea and let them walk on dry bottom of the sea so they could escape from the pharaoh's anger. After all those miracles Israelites found themselves in a desert. The desert was not their destination, but was a temporary place that they had to cross on the way to the Promised Land. My husband and I thought that we were in a temporary place also waiting for God's directions to a Promised Land.

Journey Through Life

The same way as the Israelites, we experienced many of God's miracles in our lives. God made an exodus for us from the place of heavy financial burdens to a waiting place in a desert. As we learned from the Scriptures, in order to shorten our way through desert, we had to exclude any complaints and dissatisfaction from our lives and to replace them with thanks, although it was difficult to be thankful for the trials and hardships. The Israelites were punished by God for their unlimited complaints and demands. God prolonged forty days of traveling in the desert to forty years. This was an example for us to be thankful for everything we had and ask God to shorten our waiting time. We believed that He would! God is our father, sponsor, savior and the purpose of our existence.

May everyone praise Him forever! Why doesn't God let His children have an easy and worry free life? Because we wouldn't appreciate all the blessings that God gave us. You would never graduate from school if you don't study hard for many years. You would never understand how to be a mother and how to love a child if you didn't give birth to one, going though a lot of painful moments. Doctors perform painful surgeries on their patients, not because they want to torture them, but for one good reason – to cure them from pain. God let us go through many painful moments in our lives for us to become better, nicer, healthier and more valuable.

Before I came to the United States I asked God a following question, "What am I going to do in the US?" God replied, "You will be turning millstones." I was kind of puzzled. I expected that God would tell me that I would be rich and famous and would have a comfortable life, but He didn't. He just said that I would be turning millstones! I had to accept that. From that moment I knew that things wouldn't be easy for me, but the only thing I asked Him was not to leave me alone in difficult times. I asked Him to help me through all the problems and troubles that I would meet on my way. And He did and continues to do that. I know that I will always get His support if I don't turn away from Him.

Dear reader, if you never experienced a relationship with God, it is not late today. Call Him and He will change your life. You will see how much easier it is to handle trials when you feel His powerful hand holding and supporting you in all your ways. God is not a myth, He is very real! Just give Him a chance!

XLVII. The Final Chapter Before The Conclusion

I was sitting in the church office in front of my computer thinking about the kaleidoscope of people's destinies. How wonderfully God works everything out when we turn to Him. It doesn't matter where we come from and who we are; God loves us all. It is difficult to understand His love when we lack it ourselves. We love those who love us or those who are good to us. God's love is different. He loves us with an unconditional love, which doesn't depend on who we are or what we do…

My chain of thoughts was broken by the voice of the Pastor.

"Good morning, Galina," he said, widely opening the door of my office. "You seemed to be in your imaginary world."

"Not really, I am just thinking about people's destinies."

"This life is very complicated," he said. "You never know what you could meet on your way, but it is very important to meet with Jesus."

"I know that and I am grateful to my parents that showed me a way to Jesus. But you don't have to grow up in a Christian family to be a believer. God reveals Himself to those that never heard of Him before."

"That's right," said the Pastor. "This is the purpose why we are here – to preach the Gospel."

"Of course, many that hear it - believe. "Faith comes from hearing, and hearing from the Word of God." Romans 10:17. When I was a member of the church in Pennsylvania we had a guest speaker Jimo – former voodoo priest."

"Are you kidding me?"

"Not at all. His testimony is very impressive. Do you want to hear it?"

"Please, I will be glad to," Pastor moved the chair closer to my desk and took a position of a listener.

"This is a long story, but it worth to hear it...

Jimo was a popular voodoo priest in Haiti. Not only he was famous for performing voodoo ceremonies, but also he was known and supported by the high league of Haitian government and had unlimited privileges. He was one proud and self-centered person. Many times he manipulated people around him using his power. He never took "No" for an answer. Everyone would always respond to him, "Yes, Master." Enjoying his lifestyle and all his wealth, Jimo never let anything disturb his caprice.

One day he was crossing some poor neighborhoods on his luxury car. For some reason his eyes fell on a simple girl who was walking on the sidewalk. Something in that girl got his attention. She looked pretty young and had a nice figure. She was carrying a canvas bag; probably she was coming from work and was heading to her house. Jimo slowed down and when he aligned with the girl, he rolled the window of the car down. The girl turned her head toward him, smiled and continued walking. Jimo looked closer at the girl and found that she was unusually beautiful and there was something alluring in her smile. He decided to start a conversation. "Hi, pretty lady," he said driving with the same speed as the girl walked. "My name is Jimo. Could you tell me your name?"

"Well, nice to meet you, Jimo," she said. "My name is Adline and how could I help you?"

"Help???" Jimo almost yelled in response. "No, no, I am not looking for help, I have all the help that I need. I just found that you are a very attractive young girl, why don't you come with me for a dinner? I will serve you with the best treat that you probably never got to try."

Journey Through Life

"No, thank you," she responded to him. "I have to go home and help my parents with the garden. Sorry, I cannot come with you, but I could talk to you for a few minutes."

"All right, all right," he said. "What is that you could talk to me about that I don't already know?"

"I could tell you something that is the most important in the world."

"And what is that?" Jimo was loosing his patience.

"Well, the most important in the world is our LORD JESUS CHRIST."

"Jesus Christ? What are you talking about? Who is that Jesus, that you consider so important?"

Adline told him that Jesus is the supreme power of the Universe. He is the Creator and Savior and also our best friend. She went on and on telling him the greatest things about Jesus.

"Hold on, hold on," Jimo stopped her. "How do you expect me to believe you? How would you justify everything you just told me? It sounds just like a fairytale from my grandmother's fairy book. This sounds nothing like the truth."

"Jesus is the Truth," she replied. "He is the Way, and the Truth, and the Life."

Jimo just laughed in response. He didn't believe in any of those concepts that the girl was telling him about. There was no other power than the power that he got – the voodoo power! And who is this poor girl talking to someone powerful like him, trying to convince him in the power of her Jesus? "I don't have to listen to all those nonsense stories," he said to himself. The only thing he was after – was the girl herself, but he found that it wasn't that easy to get her. She was just a "hard nut".

"All right," Adline interrupted the minute of silence. "You don't seem to be interested in my subject, too bad. But if you would like to hear more about Jesus, please come and visit our church at the L'amore center."

With these words the girl slowly moved away. Jimo was frustrated of his ruined plans. He didn't like failures and this time he got nothing but failure. Not only he couldn't convince the girl to go out with him, but also she told him something that hurt his pride. More than anything in the world he wanted to prove his voodoo power, therefore he made a plan. "I am not going to leave this subject alone!" he said, slowly following the girl to her house.

On the following day after his voodoo ceremony Jimo went home and started preparations for his secret operation. He packed drugs, balms, potions, and all the necessities for that "special project". That night he went to the house where that strange girl lived. The house was all dark, there was not a singe light near it and that's what Jimo needed. Stealthily he approached the house and pushed the window on the back wall. It didn't take him long to open the window. He quietly got into the house, carrying his "valuables" along with him. After some time he found the room where Adline was peacefully sleeping in her bed. She had no idea of the danger that was approaching her. Jimo came to the bed and stood there in a silence, sorting out his strategies. Making sure that it was quiet all around he proceeded with his ceremony. He closed his eyes and made a "prayer"; probably you couldn't call it a prayer, but something like a calling for the devil. Then he opened his suitcase and pulled a bottle that contained a "magic" powder. Actually it was just a very strong drug that could freeze a person's muscles on the touch and make the person a "living mummy". Jimo opened the bottle and raised his hand up, trying to drop the powder on the girl's forehead, when all of a sudden, he heard a strong voice, "Don't touch her, she is my child!" Jimo jumped away in fear, he almost dropped the drug on his own hand! He quickly looked around, but everything was calm and quiet

Journey Through Life

as it was few minutes ago. Jimo decided that it was probably just in his head. He lifted the bottle with the "magic" powder again, focusing on the peaceful face of the girl. He tilted the bottle slowly just above the girl's forehead, but something stopped his hand. "What happened, why is my hand getting numb?" he asked himself. "I hope that I didn't drop any of this mixture on it!" He tried to switch hands, but was paralyzed by the powerful voice that filled the room again, "Don't touch her, she is my daughter! If you try to touch her one more time, you will fall dead right where you stand!" The voice was so powerful with such an authority, that Jimo froze. When he came out of the state of shock, he quickly looked around and not seeing anyone grabbed his items and ran out of the house through the same window that he came in.

All kinds of questions puzzled his mind that night. He was convinced that he heard a supernatural voice but he didn't have any explanations for that. He never experienced anything like that in his entire life. All scared and confused Jimo was trying to fall asleep, but the voice still sounded in his ears and he couldn't get rid of it. He was twisting and turning in his bed in a cold sweat, but never could find even a minute of sleep.

On the next day he drove back to Adline's house. Patiently and anxiously he waited for hours with the full head of questions. Soon he saw the girl walking home just like the other day. She was very surprised to see Jimo again.

"Did you forget to tell me something, sir?" she asked friendly. But when she looked at him closer she saw that he was troubled for some reason. She didn't find the same proud face as she remembered from two days ago. Instead, he looked scared and worried.

"Is everything all right, sir?" she asked again.

"I am not sure," he responded. "I guess, you have to help me out this time. Does this powerful Jesus, that you mentioned the other day, live in your house?"

"Of course," she replied. "He lives in my heart and in my house and in the whole Universe. And if you would invite Him, He will also live in your heart and in your house."

Jimo was kind of confused, he couldn't quite understand what Adline was telling him. But he knew that she had some kind of supernatural power on her side, which was stronger than any of his voodoo practices. After a short silence he decided to make a confession about the events that happened to him last night. With his eyes fixed on the ground he told her everything that he experienced yesterday. Then he concluded,

"I am so sorry, I thought that I had all the powers in my hands. But now I got the knowledge of something that is much more powerful than anything I ever had. I am very sorry that I wanted to hurt you but I am glad that your Jesus protected you from a criminal like me. Please forgive me and ask your Jesus to forgive me too. I don't know if your Jesus could love people like me, but I know that He loves you very much. I don't know how to cleanse my sins but I wish that one day I could find your Jesus!"

Tears ran down his cheeks, he wasn't ashamed anymore to cry in front of this young and poor girl. Adline was touched by Jimo's confession and she almost cried too. But then she wiped her eyes with a handkerchief and said,

"Please come to my church on Sunday morning and you will hear the good news that you never heard before. I promise that you will meet with Jesus, well, you met Him already – you heard His voice."

Adline told him that Jesus died for all sinners and He forgives everyone who comes to Him. He cleansed our sins by His blood and He never remembers them again.

Journey Through Life

After that conversation with Adline Jimo felt much better. He felt like the whole New World just opened in front of him. He was still anxious but not as scared anymore, he experienced the happiness that filled his heart. Today his eyes opened to see something new and exciting that he never saw before. He felt that he just woke up from the voodoo hypnosis, falsely believing in the powers that never existed. How could he devote all his life to a simple devil's lie! He was robbed and cheated and everything that he believed and worshipped, was just a dirty pile of trash. For the first time in his life he removed dark sunglasses from his eyes and realized how bright was the sun and how beautiful was everything created by God! The meaning of life and the sense of living became clear to him. "Oh, God! I was lost but You found me. I was blind but You opened my eyes! I was deaf but You opened my ears and spoke to me! I want to know You better, Jesus! You, who gave light to my eyes and breath to my lungs. I want to be one of Your servants, I want to worship Your name until the day of my death. Please accept me, Jesus, if You can. Please forgive me all the evil deeds that I have done to other people. Please, forgive me…"

Jimo was sitting at the empty table. He didn't see anything around him, he couldn't think of anything else, but this powerful Jesus, who was introduced to him by Adline. In the deepest thoughts he completely forgot about the time of the day and his missed dinner. Nothing made sense any more except unknown Jesus. Then he started to think of all his wasted days, weeks, years of his life, life of stealing, cheating and hurting others. It was a worthless life, full of sin. Suddenly, the fear filled his heart. "What if Jesus will find out what kind of life I lived and rejects me? How will I convince Him that I am not the same anymore? I don't have a single evidence of anything good that I ever did! Will Jesus believe me that I changed? Will He give me another chance to start all over? But even if He does, what am I going to do with all these years that convict me to sin and death?... Oh, Jesus! Please don't reject me! I really want to start my life all over! Please help me establish this new beginning!" Loud sobbings burst out of Jimo's chest. He felt like a convicted felony, which was just acquitted by The King, although he didn't deserve a bit of it. Repentance, regrets, disappointments mixed together with the feeling of love and forgiveness of Jesus created a hurricane of tears, that pored like two rivers out of his eyes. He just let it go...

With all these confused feelings of hopelessness and confession Jimo fell deeply asleep right at the table. He didn't remember how reality changed into a dream. In his dream he was walking on a muddy road, full of pits and swamps. But being too busy looking at himself in the mirror he never noticed the surroundings. He never noticed how the stains of the mud stuck to his clothes and body. Neither he noticed tiny pieces of dust that he picked up on the way. He just walked on the road and enjoyed looking in the mirror. All of a sudden, he heard a voice, strong like a thunder and powerful like a storm, calling his name. Jimo stopped and shockingly looked around, but didn't see anybody, except the empty road. Then he heard the voice again,

"Jimo, Jimo..." The voice was coming from above.

"Yes," Jimo responded. "Who are you and how do you know my name?"

The voice replied, "I am Jesus, whom you just discovered and whom you are trying to reach. Look at yourself and tell me what you see?"

When Jimo looked at himself in the mirror again, he saw a homeless person, dressed in dirty rags.

"Jesus, I am sorry, I never knew that I am in such poverty and also very unclean." The voice responded, "I opened your eyes because you asked me and now you can see who you actually are. I heard your prayers and I know all the fears

Journey Through Life

that trouble your heart. Your soul was like these dirty rags that picked up all the dirt of this world. You were swimming in the mud, thinking that you are the star. But now you realized how poor and blind was your soul. And since you asked me, I am going to cleanse you and make you whiter and brighter than snow. My blood that I shed from the cross cleansed all your sins and now you are free from your old sinful ways. Go ahead and sin no more. Testify to others about my Name and be my servant and my Son!"

When the voice stopped talking, Jimo looked at himself again and saw that his clothes were bright like a pearl and there wasn't even one stain on it. Jimo yelled with the full voice,

"Jesus, here I am, your servant, your son! Thank you for accepting me in the army of your soldiers! I will praise Your name forever, Jesus!"

Jimo woke up... He found himself sleeping on the table, but there was not even a sign of fear left in his heart. His heart was filled with unusually sweet happiness, which he never experienced before in his life. He had no doubt that Jesus visited him in his dream and gave him all the answers that he was looking for. Jimo became a newborn Christian.

On Sunday morning Jimo anxiously got up, quickly got dressed and ran to the car. He decided to get to the church as soon as possible. He came there so early that the door was still locked. He knocked a few times and someone let him in. Jimo sat on the bench by himself, full of new and unusual feelings, like the freshman soldier, joining the army of Christ. The church was filling slowly and soon the service started. Everybody greeted Jimo with a friendly smile, Jimo could see that the Christian love was written on their faces. Then the choir rose and started to sing the first hymn. When the sounds of the hymn filled the church, Jimo felt like the windows of the heaven opened on the top of his head. The music was touching Jimo's heart and soon he sang along with the choir. He simply couldn't be silent! Although he didn't know the words of the song, the song was coming out of his heart. He was imagining that he joined the choir of angels; how beautiful was that heavenly song! Jimo didn't remember how long the worship service lasted but he enjoyed every moment of it. He wished that he could freeze that moment of happiness and joy.

Meanwhile, the service was rolling on and soon the pastor came up to the podium and spoke about Good News from the Bible. Jimo was swallowing every word of the pastor, trying to memorize as much scripture as he could. At the end of the speech pastor invited everyone, who would like to accept Jesus in his heart, to come forward. When Jimo heard the invitation, he got up from the bench and ran to the stage. He felt that he didn't want to be late telling everybody how wonderfully Jesus rescued him from his wicked ways. He got to the podium and grabbed the microphone from the pastor's hand. He put all his emotions in his testimony and grasped the full attention of the congregation. He saw tears on most of the faces; he saw the impressions of surprise and happiness. He continued to testify...

Finally his eyes fell on a pretty girl, who was sitting in the middle row near the entrance door. The girl's eyes were watery from tears, but for some reasons tears didn't make her face look sad. On the contrary, it was glowing with some unusual light. He would recognize this face out of a million; it was his angel-stranger Adline. This beautiful stranger led him to salvation and made a bridge for him to the land of Jesus. "How am I going to repay her for this wonderful revelation? Her words changed my whole life and the whole meaning of it! My eyes had opened and now I know my destiny!" All these thoughts came through his head at the moment when he saw Adline.

He stopped speaking for a few seconds and then he continued, "Dear congregation, now I can call you brothers

Journey Through Life

and sisters. There is one lovely person among you, who is the reason of my spiritual birth. Adline, please come forward and please join me in a prayer of thanks. We have a lot to tell Him and a lot to praise Him for! Especially for the miracle of converting a lost and wild son into a serving one."

Adline slowly got up from the bench and moved toward the stage. She walked smoothly and quietly like she was afraid to disturb that powerful testimony. The pastor and the elders joined Jimo and Adline in a prayer. During the prayer Jimo felt a presence of power similar to the power of electricity flowing through his body. He knew that this was the touch of the hand of Jesus over him and he felt safe.

After this wonderful day of the very first church visit, Jimo finally understood that he belong there. Total peace and satisfaction came into his heart. Jimo and Adline became best friends. They often got together to read and discussed God's Word in the Bible. Due to years of experience in Christianity, Adline became a great Christian teacher for him and later his wife. Jimo and Adline became a team of great ministers.

They travel a lot and visit many churches, sharing their miraculous testimony with others. They bring the word of life to many non-believers, trying to shed light in their lives. Many accepted Jesus after hearing Jimo's and Adline's story."

The story impressed the Pastor very much. He thanked me for sharing it with him and said, "I wish I could meet this couple, I would shower them with questions. I was always curious about voodoo religion and what makes them believe in their evil powers." He got up from the chair and walked out in the door.

I remained in the office alone. I was brainstorming the Pastor's comments. "That's right, what make people follow evil... or good? There will always be two powers: good & evil. They are always in a battle. But I am so blessed to grow up in the family that taught me everything good and the source of good is God. I learned about God since my very early childhood and will never regret it. God is the real power and He illustrated it to me numerous times. He always walked with me in my long journey – JOURNEY THROUGH LIFE."

XLVIII. Conclusion

Dear reader, the events that I described in this book, are not fiction, but real stories that I experienced in my life or I know that happened in lives of others. The main purpose and idea of this book is to show you how God miraculously works in lives of those people who need Him and who opened their hearts to Him. If I wanted to describe all the details of walking with God and all the answers that I received from Him, it wouldn't fit in a book. But everything is written in the Book of Life, whose author and keeper is God Himself. God is the initiator of life. He is the creator of people and He is everything that is good, fair and beautiful. He is Alpha and Omega, the beginning and the end. There is no other explanation to the existence and meaning of life. No matter how hard scientists thought for years trying to explain the existence of human nature, all of the theories failed. Because there is only one answer to this question: God is All-powerful creator, who designed the Human being and everything under the sun.

Do you know, my friend, who you are serving? Maybe you are not aware of that but the truth is that if you are not serving God, then you are serving Satan. There is no neutral position, is it one or the other. If you already accepted Jesus in your heart, you will spend an eternity with Jesus, and this is an absolute truth! Otherwise, Satan, the deceiver will trick you into eternal lake of fire, which is called hell. Satan has accomplished throughout history all evil things: he lied, he robbed, he killed, destroyed, and he failed.

And when any of us rejects God's authority in any area of our lives, the outcome is as certain as betting on yesterday's football game!

We will be deceived,
We will be robbed,
We will be killed,

We will be destroyed,
We will not succeed.

One day Jesus said when the Pharisees tried to keep Him away from the city, "Today and tomorrow I am forcing demons out and healing people. Then on the third day, I will reach my goal." (Luke 13:32). That is a prophetic statement as well as a historic one. David wrote in Psalm 90:4, "To you, a thousand years is like the passing of a day, or like a few hours in the night (Ps. 90:4).

A thousand years is as a day. Today and tomorrow – two days. Two thousand years. The power of the Gospel has covered the earth, and on the third day the Messiah will be glorified in His thousand-year reign on earth, the Millennium. We are coming to the end of the second day. And the third day is forming just below the horizon; it will dawn with the appearing of Messiah, the Anointed One who will be sent by God to inaugurate the final redemption at the end of days.

What then shall we do?

Apostle Peter wrote, "This makes us more sure about the message the prophets gave. It is good for you to follow closely what they said as you would follow a light shining in a dark place, until the day begins and the morning star rises in your hearts. Most of all, you must understand this: no prophecy in the Scriptures ever come from the prophet's own interpretation. No prophecy ever came from what a person wanted to say, but people led by the Holy Spirit spoke words from God." (2 Pet. 1:19-21).

Peter testified in this passage that the accounts of the life, miracles, death, and resurrection of Jesus Christ, are not just made up stories. Peter and the other disciples saw Jesus. They touched Him, ate with Him, talked to Him – they even saw Him ascend into heaven. They were eyewitnesses of his majesty. Peter himself, a Jewish man well-acquainted with the writings of the prophets, saw how the Lord Jesus fulfilled

Journey Through Life

the prophecies of the Old Testament. And he was convinced that just as Jesus fulfilled the prophecies concerning His first coming, He would fulfill the prophecies of the times yet to come.

My dear friends, if you remember nothing else about this book, please grasp with your head and your heart this overpowering truth from the Word of God – we are the terminal generation. We are the ones who need to prepare today for our ever after. Like no other generation, we are the ones who cannot take for granted tomorrow. We must not put off until tomorrow spiritual decisions and spiritual actions, which can be done today.

If you are a believer in Jesus the Messiah, lift up your head and rejoice, for your redemption is drawing near. Too many Christians are living as if they're going to be here forever. To them the words of Jesus shine, like a warning beacon, "The Good News about God's kingdom will be preached in all the world, to every nation. Then the end will come." (Matt. 24:14).

If you have not yet trusted Jesus Christ as Messiah, the signs of the times should compel you to recognize that the hand of God is moving in the city of Jerusalem and in the nation of Israel. The Messiah is soon to come. If you listen closely, you can hear the footsteps of the Messiah walking through the clouds of heaven. You can hear the thundering hoofbeats of the four horsemen of the Apocalypse as even now they pick up speed, racing to their destiny on the fields of Armageddon.

If this book outlives my time on earth, let me assure you that it is not too late to recognize Jesus Christ as the Son of God, the promised Messiah. He is truly King of Kings and Lord of Lords; and He wants to bring you life abundant on earth and life eternal in the world to come. He extends to you the opportunity to escape the coming time of trial.

Like two-faced Janus of old, we will soon see the advent of two Messiahs: one false, one true.
Which one will you choose?

XLIX. A Prayer for You

Father, I ask you to bless my friends reading this book right now. I am asking You to minister to their spirit at this very moment. Where there is pain, give them Your peace and mercy. Where there is self-doubting, release a renewed confidence in Your ability to work through them.

Where there is tiredness, or exhaustion, I ask You to give them understanding, patience, and strength as they learn submission to Your leading. Where there is spiritual stagnation, I ask You to renew them by revealing Your nearness, and by drawing them into greater intimacy with You.

Where there is fear, reveal Your love, and release to them to Your courage. Where there is a sin blocking them, reveal it, and break its hold over my friend's life. Bless their finances, give them greater vision, and raise up leaders, and friends to support, and encourage them. Give each of them discernment to recognize the evil forces around them, and reveal to them the power they have in You to do these things in Jesus name. Amen.

About the Author

Galina and her family have been a huge influence and blessing in my life and ministry. Soon after joining our church Galina became the Pastor's secretary! Usually, a pastor teaches his flock. But Galina ended up teaching her pastor many valuable spiritual lessons, I learned from Galina the need for God's servants to be sensitive to the leading of the Holy Spirit, and to immediately obey His prompting. She modeled that in her life, and I am forever grateful that she demonstrated that sensitivity to God's leading.

She also taught me how to be a better multi-cultural pastor. Galina is from Belarus. Her husband is from Haiti. Together, they have maintained their own cultural interests, and yet have blended their cultures together into a joyful, understanding, and loving family. Our church was multicultural before the Cherubins arrived. But the Cherubins personified the message that we tried to convey as a church family...that you don't have to stop being who you are culturally in order to fit into a church.

Another great lesson that Galina taught me is that, even in times of pressure and stress, it is okay to laugh and enjoy life. In some of the most high stress times in our church office, Galina would say something that would produce such laughter and joy that made the problems seem more tolerable.

God certainly blessed Galina with great intelligence, but also with great wit and humor! Galina is one of the most godly, spiritually minded women I have ever met. When she shares with you what God has taught her in life, you need to listen. Her life is filled with ups and downs, spiritual battles, and moments of great victories. She continues to this day seeking to please God above all else. Thank you, Galina, for being such a wonderful friend and teacher to your pastor!

    Sincerely,
    John A, Norris
    Pastor of Riverside Baptist Church
    Decatur, Illinois

Printed in the United States
42451LVS00001B/17